REFUTATION OF THE KORAN

ISBN: 1452867836
EAN-13: 9781452867830

Title: "Refutation of the Koran"
Subtitle: "translated by Londini Ensis"
Author: Riccoldo of Monte Croce OP

Self-Published
© Londini Ensis 2010

For permissions or to contact the translator
E-mail: londiniensis@live.com

RICCOLDO OF MONTE CROCE OP

REFUTATION OF THE KORAN

TRANSLATED BY LONDINI ENSIS

For David & Nigel

May God Protect You Always

CONTENTS

PREFACE TO THE NEW EDITION

I completed this translation a while ago, as the following preface will inform the reader, but it has become quite evident to me that I will not have time to revise it to a professional standard over the coming years. The new technology of print-on-demand publication, however, at least affords me this opportunity to make my work available cheaply to the world-wide scholarly community, and I hope that it will be of at least some benefit to those who are interested.

Readers should be aware (as I was not when I was translating eight years ago) of the existence of a critical edition of *Contra Legem Saracenorum* (the original Latin text) by J.-M. Mérigoux, in *Mémorie Dominicane* 17 (1986), 1-144. The English-speaking scholarly community would perhaps still benefit from a translation directly from this edition. It seems to me, though, that the edition from which I translated, that is, the equivalent of the 1507 Basel edition, must continue to hold some interest for scholars of the work's reception. In consideration of the work's influence during the Reformation and Modern Era, it is important to bear in mind the simultaneous existence of the different editions and to be aware of which is being used by whom, should the differences prove significant.

Since I first stumbled upon this text in Luther's Works, it seemed fitting that I also include as an appendix to this little book a translation of Luther's preface to the first edition of the Koran, which I also translated from the Latin in 2002. May all this be received in the same good will by which it is offerred. I realise that this is no scholarly work and it stands without peer review. So when scholarship supercedes its mark, let all copies be consigned to the fire and let it be forgotten as the embarrassing vestige of an immature youth. For now, it is yours to read.

Londini Ensis, 2010

PREFACE

This *Refutation of the Koran* was first written by a man called Riccoldo Pennini, from San Pier Maggiore in the Tuscan village of Monte Croce. He was born in 1243. Like his brothers Domenico, Bencivenni and Sinibaldo, he joined the Dominican Order, entering the Dominican monastery of Santa Maria Novella in Florence in 1267, taking his vows in 1268. From 1272 he taught at the Dominican convents of Pisa, Prato and Lucca, and subsequently became a famous preacher in Florence.

In 1286, Brother Riccoldo was given a papal commission to preach in Acre, Palestine, and so in the late summer of 1288 he landed at Acre. Having travelled throughout Palestine, he continued his missionary journeys, going through Erzerum, Ararat, and staying in Tabriz for the winter of 1289-1290. Then after visiting Mosul and Tekrit, he went to Baghdad, where he stayed for several years. He was there when Acre fell to Muslim forces and when Christian captives were being sold on the slave market. He suffered deep depression after learning of the demise of the fellow members of his order there. However, he was soon forced to leave Baghdad because of the persecution of Christians (that came about after Ghazan Khan's conversion to Islam in 1294) and he travelled around disguised as a camel driver, returning to Florence around 1300. There he gained prominence until, in 1315, he was made prior of Santa Maria Novella, and died on 31st October, 1320.

This Refutation is a result of brother Riccoldo's time spent in Baghdad, as well as other places, where he learned Arabic and acquired his knowledge of the Koran by speaking with the Islamic teachers there. It has had an interesting history; probably far more interesting than we know.

Demetrius Cydonius, a Byzantine theologian, translated the work into Greek in an effort to find spiritual weapons against Islam at the time when the Turks threatened to become a danger to the Byzantine empire (1360s).

The Confutation was then used by the Byzantine emperors John VI Cantacuzenos (1347-54) and Manuel II Palaiologos (1391-1425) in their dealings with Islam.

Nicholas of Cusa (1401-1464) also approved the work, mentioning it in his *Cribratio Alcorani* (1461).

Bartholomaeus de Monte Arduo used Demetrius' Greek translation and translated it back into Latin. He dedicated the work to King Ferdinand the Catholic for reasons that can be read in Bartholomaeus' letter to Ferdinand, which is included in this English translation.

The reformer Martin Luther first came into contact with the confutation around 1530. For a long time, this, and Nicholas of Cusa's *Cribratio Alcorani* (mentioned above), were Luther's only source of knowledge about the Koran. He read the Confutation many times, but was at first reluctant to believe that Riccoldo had described Islam correctly. Luther wrote, "I have read the book of Brother Richard, of the order of Preachers, which is called *Confutatio Alcorani*, several times. I cannot believe that there are reasonable people on earth who can be persuaded by the devil to believe such terrible things." However, at the February carnival of 1542, Luther was first able to read the Koran in Latin, and judge for himself. As a result he translated Riccoldo's work into German and it was published in April 1542. The Koran itself was published in Latin the following year, with a preface also written by Luther.

This English translation was done by working from Bartholomaeus de Monte Arduo's Latin, the same Latin from which Luther translated into German. The Latin can also be found in the Weimar edition of *Luther's Works*, Vol. 53, pg. 273-387. In other words, this is not a translation of Riccoldo's original text, but of Bartholomaeus' translation of Demetrius' translation of Riccoldo's text. Having said this, the Weimar edition does include some helpful footnotes giving variations from Riccoldo's original text, as well as from other editions, to make translation easier. To my knowledge, this is the first English translation of Brother Riccoldo's *Refutation of the Koran*.

The English text has been split up into paragraphs for general ease of reading. Some points, though not all, at which I have done this were where Luther has done the same with his German.

Foot-notes have also been added where I thought they might be more helpful than none, though they are not included in the Latin itself. Again, some of these footnotes are drawn from the Weimar edition's German notes.

The general reader should note that this translation has not been carried out by any expert, while the reader educated in Latin will recognise this immediately. There was, in my mind, a great need for this document to be published in the English language, since it is a document of such historical significance. With this in mind, I hope that the benefit of the availability of this text in English may go a little way towards inclining readers to forgive me for the errors contained therein.

As for criticism of brother Riccoldo's confutation and his arguments, far be it from me to make judgements concerning the value or validity of anything put forward by such a great scholar. That, I might suggest, is for the reader to decide.

Londini Ensis, 2002

Refutation of the Koran

Or the Law of the Saracens

Recently Translated from Greek into Latin

Bartholemaeus de Monte Arduo, of Picenum, sends many greetings to Ferdinand King of Argonia and Sicily.

Demetrius of Crete, a man most skilled in both languages, has translated the work of brother Riccoldo of the Order of Preachers[1] from Latin to Greek. I did not for that reason, most fair and universal King, want to translate it back from Greek into Latin. Nor because I did not think that such a work existed amongst the Latin speakers,[2] but since I saw that Demetrius the Cretan had translated that piece from Latin to Greek quite elegantly. For that reason, according to my abilities, I have tried to translate that work again into our language with the same elegance of speech and to bring it back in a more polished form and a clearer style as best as I could.

To you, most fair and universal King, it is rightly dedicated. You alone amongst the kings of the Christians have inflicted at this time the greatest disasters upon the Mohammedan school. For it was no small amount of praise that you earned for yourself when you brought back Betica[3] into the power of Christendom, a province that had practised the Mohammedian faith for eight hundred years. Even now you intend to take the whole of Africa, which you will be able to gain with ease, since those peoples are unfit for war at the moment, seeing that they have not been accustomed to long-term fighting with Christians. For it was more difficult for you to storm the province of Betica than it will be for you to liberate the whole of Africa in your power. For those soldiers in Betica were most vigorous and accustomed to continual warring with the Spain. But these men, on the other hand, are yellow bellied and give up faster, since they put aside their custom of fighting with the Christian name a long time ago. Nor are they practised in war like those who once set upon Spain and Italy led by Hannibal. Nor do they have that force of arms which a Spanish soldier,

---

[1] ...of Preachers: in other words, Dominican.

[2] Nor...speakers: In other words: And I was well aware that such a work already existed amongst the Latin Speakers.

[3] The province of southern Spain that includes Cordoba and Granada.

both vigorous and highly experienced in war, is said to have. There are also plenty of great works there, by which the spirits of soldiers are inflamed with hope of very great booty. Everything will proceed to please you, if you follow through with the rest of the war that has begun. Nor is it something for you to fear that war will be taken to Spain by someone, particularly at this new time for you, considering your union with the most Christian king of the Franks since a treaty was entered into.

Therefore, follow through with the war that has begun and take all your men over to Africa, which you will easily be able to bring under the yoke. Indeed, once that has been conquered and brought back under the power of Christendom, then you will easily regain Jerusalem, a land so great, so fertile, so holy, yet which is obedient at this time to the Sultan of Baghdad. However, those who currently defend that homeland are slaves bought when they are young from far-reaching provinces, and these men certainly do not amount to twenty thousand men who, since they were forced to leave the Christian religion, now follow the Mohammedan sect. The remainder are actually Saracens who are subjected by them. We can deduce how soft and effeminate they are from this, that they are never allowed to take up arms nor mount a horse nor are they allowed to do anything manly, but they work either in agriculture or commerce or another base employment of similar stature. Since that is so, no-one doubts that you will very easily gain from that expedition a most triumphant victory as well as the holy city Jerusalem, in which our Saviour the Lord Jesus Christ announced the Gospel and put in place for us the new testament. This city you will free from the frightful and excessive religion of the Mohammedans. Once you have carefully read this confutation of Brother Riccoldo, then you will learn for the first time how empty this religion is, how worthless, how lacking in substance; and how it has nothing of importance to say for our present day. Farewell.

A CONFUTATION OF THE WIDE-SPREAD LAW OF THE SARACENS BY THE ACCURSED MOHAMMED

TRANSLATED FROM THE ROMAN LANGUAGE INTO GREEK BY
DEMETRIUS OF CRETE, THEN TRANSLATED BACK FROM GREEK INTO
LATIN BY BARTHOLEMAEUS DE MONTE ARDUO OF PICENUM

OF RICCOLDO OF THE ORDER OF BROTHERS KNOWN AMONGST
THE LATINS AS THE PREACHERS.

"How many are the days of your servant? When will you execute judgement on them that persecute me? The proud have told me vain tales which are not after your law, O Lord. All your commandments are faithful: they persecute me wrongfully."[4] These are the words of a church at war, weeping and groaning that it is burdened with all kinds of wretchedness, liberation from which relies completely on divine aid. But although the church has endured countless sufferings and grief, yet all these should be brought together into the following three headings:

Firstly, it most clearly endured the rage of persecution brought to it by ungodly tyrants. Moreover, this happened on the largest scale, from the time when Christ suffered up to the time of Constantine, that is, for three hundred and ten years. During this time, the Romans, who held a monopoly of power, killed countless holy martyrs of God as well as an endless record of others everywhere around the world. David, who feels compassion for this time, says for the church: "How many are

---

[4] Psalm 118:84 (Vulgate) or Psalm 119 *Kaph* (English).

the days of your servant? When will you execute judgement on them that persecute me?" But since the bloodshed of the saints cried out to God and they themselves gleamed with miracles, suddenly there was a turning to the right hand of the Most High, and those who had previously been Christians' persecutors built churches and were made leaders of the war against the impious.

But immediately a second persecution of heretics rose up. For suddenly the bloody Devil appeared, roaring out of his scales and hissing all kinds of heresies – namely of Arius,[5] Sabellius,[6] Macedonius[7] and other heretics, for which at the greatest time David said, "The proud have told me vain tales, which are not after your law, O Lord." But then the light of the teaching of the church was brought out and set down when many teachers then appeared and opened up the divine scriptures. Hilary[8] was such a man, Augustine,[9] Jerome[10] and Gregory[11] and a multitude of holy fathers rose up, who lived most excellent and most sound lives in the wildernesses, so much so that the mouth of the Devil was bound by the weak and common flax. In this way, the mouths of those speaking in an unjust way about the scriptures were covered.

But immediately afterwards, this third corruption became strong in the churches, namely, a danger coming from deceitful brothers. Whereby immediately after the time of Gregory, affliction strengthened its grip through corrupt men on the hypocrisy of those who speak falsehood. And so many lies and fabrications were born again to life, concerning doctrine and righteousness, that many men lowered themselves and helped the unjust and the tyrants. For these men fell forward into such

---

[5] Arius: held that Christ is not true, natural, eternal God. Hence, Arianism denies the co-eternity and co-essentiality of Christ with God. Condemned by the 325 Council of Nicea.
[6] Sabellius: leader of a heresy concerning the trinity known as Modalistic Monarchianism. Excommunicated for this in 220.
[7] Macedonius: considered the Holy Ghost to be only a creature and inferior to the Son. This heresy was condemned by the 381 First Council of Constantinople.
[8] St. Hilary of Poitiers (300-367), opposed Arianism vehemently.
[9] St. Augustine of Hippo (354-430).
[10] St. Jerome (340-420), also became a friend of St Gregory.
[11] St Gregory of Nazianzus (325-389).

foolishness and crookedness; they would deceive most excellent men and humiliate them. This corruption is one which will endure against the church age after age, with the result that there is not at all any hope left apart from divine aid and perseverance for the truth. From this David also says for these times: "All your commands are faithful: they persecute me wrongfully; help thou me."[12] As if saying: though the truth has been struck low for a while, it is right, however, to squeeze out this truth most vigorously and for it to be known with effect, with God's aid assisting us greatly.

Therefore, in this third state of affairs, that is, after the time of blessed Gregory in the times of Heraclius,[13] a certain man, the first born devil of Satan, rose in rebellion against the truth and the church of God. A man inclined to sexual desire and given to deceitful devices, he was called Mohammed. With the purpose and help of he who is a liar and the father of lies, he composed a law (which is unjust and full of lies), as though it were uttered from God's own mouth, indeed, a law he has called the Koran – namely, a collection of divine commandments. This Mohammed has persecuted the church of God above all others who were or ever will be. For he has not struck the church in only one way, but in three most universal ways. Now by means of a savage tyrant, in another way through deceitfulness in its laws, and again, by corrupting those who are more simple minded through his pretence of sanctity. This has had the result that they have subjected a large part of the world to his deception, by God's permission, who is frightening in his purposes for the sons of men.

I, therefore, the least in the order of Preachers, feeling compassion for such a destructive deception, considered my ways and I changed the direction of my feet towards the testimonies of God. From there, since I travelled across many seas and deserted places, also discovering Baghdad (the famous city of the Saracens, where they have among them all the

---

[12] Psalm 119:86
[13] Heraclius: Byzantine emperor 610-641.

greatest scholarly works), and there learning their letters and the Arabic language and similarly, arguing most diligently and continuously with their teachers, I understood more and more the depravity of the above mentioned law. As I was also beginning to translate this law into Latin, I found at the same time so many fabrications, lies and blasphemies and uninterrupted fiction through it all that I became full of sadness. And for that reason I decreased the amount of those letters I was writing to the church triumphant about such blasphemies as I lamented greatly in that bitter state of mind. Now, however, I intend, trusting in the truth, to expose the chief and principal lies of this unjust law and to show the matter to other brothers, with the help of which they can more easily call the followers of this heresy back to God. However, so that this happens in an orderly way, I have found that it is better to divide the whole treatise into separate chapters.

The first chapter contains the principle errors of this law.

Second: the way these errors can serve us.

Third: the fact that this law is not God's law, because neither the Old nor the New Testament bear witness to this. Also the fact that the Saracens must obey the words of the Old Testament and the Gospel.

Fourth: the fact that it does not agree in style or manner with other writers.

Fifth: that it does not agree with anything else in its opinions.

Sixth: that it contradicts itself in many ways.

Seventh: that it is not confirmed by any miracle.

Eighth: that it is irrational.

Ninth: that it contains obvious lies.

Tenth: that it is violent.

Eleventh: that it is disorderly.
Twelfth: that it is unjust.
Thirteenth: about the establishing of the Koran and who the author and inventor of this law was.

Fourteenth: about the most shameless feigning of visions.

Fifteenth: about six general points of question in the Koran and about Christ's perfection according to Mohammed.

Sixteenth: about the perfection of the Gospel according to the Koran.

Seventeenth: about the Saracens' reply to what is said above.

CHAPTER ONE. ABOUT THE PRINCIPLE ERRORS OF THIS LAW.

It is fitting, firstly, to know the principle errors which the law of the Saracens contains, concerning those which oppose divine law to the greatest extent. It should be noted, therefore, that all the dirt of times gone by which the devil has scattered in other places here and there, he also spewed out in its entirety onto Mohammed. For this man, with Sabellius, utterly denies the Trinity. Yet he puts a dual nature on that which comes from God, which can point out in itself nothing honest or similar to that which comes from God, even though it is the basis for their whole sect. For he pretends that God's essence and His Spirit are something they are not.

Then he presents God in the Koran speaking in the plural, so that the Spirit of God itself and Christ himself are not seen to be God, but of an essence which is less than God and subject to him. He agrees in this with Arius and Eunomius:[14] he falsifies Christ to be a noble creature and rising above all other creatures. However, this opinion clearly came from the Platonists, who lied about almighty God, the Father and creator of all things, from whom they said that a certain mind flowed down in the beginning, in which there are certainly all reckoning of things and this is higher than all things. This they would call the paternal mind, and after this they would say is the spirit of the earth, and in succession to this are the remaining creatures. Therefore the things which are said about the Son of God in the scriptures, these things they incorporate into that mind. Especially, however, the fact that the holy book also calls the Son

---

[14] Eunomius: denied any substantial similarity between God the Father and God the Son, arguing that God the Father is unbegotten and therefore, the Son, being begotten of the Father, cannot be equal. Heresy condemned by the 381 First Council of Constantinople.

of God the Wisdom and Word of God. He also agrees with this opinion of Avicenna,[15] who claimed that there was a supreme intelligence before the first sky existed, an intelligence which produced the first sky and beyond which he said God was firmly set in the highest place. In this way therefore, the Arians supposed about the Son of God that he was a creation that surpassed all other creatures, the intermediate being through which God created all things.

Likewise, Mohammed also claimed that Christ was most holy and endowed with virtue above all others. However, he openly says that what is in him is above man. For he calls him the Word of God, and the Spirit of God, and the Mind of God. He thinks it completely ridiculous that Christ be called God in accordance with the truth. And to demonstrate this he uses two reasons particularly. Indeed, one is because Christ himself never claimed or said this about himself. And the other is because he himself seems to have said the opposite. On this Mohammed says that though Christians say that Christ is God, yet Christ himself said to the Jews: "Worship my God and your God, my Lord and your Lord."[16] I set this out at greater length, as everyone knows, because that which the deceitful devil could not at first accomplish in the world through Arius, this he fulfilled later through Mohammed as zealousness in the church decreased and evil grew. And in the end he will strengthen the wickedness through the antichrist, who will persuade the world that God is not real and that Christ is not the Son of God, nor even a good man. It is, therefore, the primary intention of Mohammed to persuade others that Christ is not God, nor is he the Son of God, but only a holy and wise man, and a very great prophet, born of a virgin without a father (in this he agrees with the heretic Carpocrates[17]).

---

[15] Avicenna: (980-1037) Arabian physician and philosopher. His philosophy consisted of a mix of Aristotelianism and neo-Platonism.

[16] From John 20:17, "I am returning to my Father and your Father, to my God and your God."

[17] Carpocrates: Alexandrian philosopher and founder (circa 130) of a Gnostic sect that, amongst other heretical beliefs, held Christ to be one among many wise men.

Similarly, he affirms that it is impossible for God to have a son, based on the reasoning that he does not have a wife (agreeing again with the same heretic in this also). And he adds that if God did have a son, the whole world would now be in danger, as though there would have to be a difference of opinion between them. In this he agrees with the Jews and with the heretic Cerdonius.[18] And he further adds that Christ was neither killed nor crucified by the Jews, but that someone else was killed who was like him. In this he agrees with the Manichaeists.[19] And he also adds that God summoned him to himself and that he will appear again at the end of the world and will kill the antichrist, but after this, God will make Christ die. However, whoever denies the suffering of Christ, that person denies all the mysteries of the church which draw their effectiveness from the divine suffering. In this he agrees with the Donatist[20] heretics.

Then he also says that demons can be saved through the Koran and that many of them, when they heard this, were made Saracens (here following in another way the source who says that there will be demons who will be saved).

He also says that he himself ascended to God, when God sent Gabriel for him and that God placed His hand on him and that such a great feeling of rigidity began in his body when God was touching him, that it passed right through to the middle of his back's spine. In these parts it is clear that he is united with the Anthropomorphists,[21] who were used to a corporeal God. And he says that the Holy Spirit is a creature, agreeing with Macedonius. In the parts, however, where he says that the angels were made demons when they refused to worship Adam

---

[18] Cerdonius: taught that the world and the flesh are evil and that two gods exist. The good god is unknown. The evil god is the Jewish God who created the world and the flesh.
[19] Manichaeism: the 3rd century Persian synthesis of various systems of belief including, amongst others, Zoroastrianism dualism, gnosticism and some elements of Christianity.
[20] Donatist: are more often referred to as a schismatic group. They broke away from the Catholic Church in 312 and flourished in Africa until declining in the 5th century.
[21] Anthropomorphism: the ascription to the Supreme Being of the form, organs, operations, and general characteristics of human nature.

at God's command, he does not seem to be imitating anyone in this.

Furthermore he tells tall stories, saying that the greatest blessedness for men is in immoderation and pleasures, and in costly clothes, and watered gardens, agreeing in these parts with the heretic Cerinthus[22] and the same old faithless people. He also says that circumcision should be practised, endorsing the teachings of the heretic Eunomius.

He also permits a great number of wives in marriage and the seduction of slave-girls and however many one can take away while plundering in war, even taking the wives of others without concern (following in these teachings the Nicolaitan[23] heretics). Then he says that everyone who does not submit to this law should be killed unless they ransom themselves with a tribute.

And he seems to condone sodomy in men and women in the chapter about the cow, though their successors cover this up with more honourable statements.

Moreover, his whole intention is to cut short whatever was difficult to believe or hard to perform, but also to permit (the Arabs most of all) everything to which they were inclined, which are taken up by present day peoples, namely greediness, plunder and licentiousness. About virtues, however, such as humility, patience, peace, self control or about the final end, he has said nothing worth asking about, so nothing is what I shall say about that.

Moreover, so that one cannot easily argue against any one of these lies through the Old or New Testament, or through works which philosophers have written (in which they themselves discuss excellence, sin and the final end), he ordered that nothing whatsoever was worthy of trust that was contrary to the extensive law given by him, and commanded that anyone

---

[22] Cerinthus: Gnostic founder of Adoptionism who lived during the life of St. John. Amongst other heretical beliefs, he thought lightly of sin, regarding the body as unimportant and teaching that carnal appetites could be gratified without limit or control.
[23] Nicolaitan: heresy that permits licentiousness, condemned by Revelation 2:6 and 2:15.

who dared to say something contrary to this be killed or punished with a more severe penalty. Yet he himself strongly praised the psalmist and the other prophets.

He also says many things about himself - that Christ prophesied about him in the gospel to the sons of Israel when he said: "I announce unto you the apostle of God, who is the one to come after me, and his name is Mohammed."[24]   He even affirmed that this name was written from eternity on the throne of God in that higher place at His right hand.

However, he showed not one miracle to credit this, but said, unsheathing his sword, that he was sent by God not in the excellence of miracles, but of arms.

These are the principle errors which the Koran contains, that is the law of the Saracens. However, the lies which are contained in that book are infinite to bear. We will not discuss these in any chapter.

---

[24] K. 61.6

CHAPTER TWO. HOW ONE SHOULD BE CONVERTED WITH THESE THINGS.

Secondly, it is fitting to know that they are extremely eager to hear something about our faith and especially about the Holy Trinity and incarnation. However, they do not want to believe in these things, nor can they understand them. They also do not want to believe, nor can they understand those things, because they surpass and exceed human reason and understanding. For it says in Isaiah, "If you have not believed, nor will you understand."[25] And since those teachings are contrary to the Koran, which they themselves consider most continually to be the Word of God, for that reason also they do not accept those things but mock them.

For it says in Proverbs that the foolish man does not accept wise words, unless you tell him things which please him.[26] So one should not put forward the holy beliefs to them right from the beginning, nor scatter pearls before the pigs,[27] but at the beginning, one should show them the falsity of their law. For it is not right to sow virtues unless the diseases are first torn out by the roots. And it is also best to choose the quickest way in all things.

However, it is easier to show that their faith is wrong than it is to demonstrate the truth of our own faith. For although their faith is something which we do not observe, ours is a gift of God. Indeed, our faith proves strongly to be in accordance with the genuine commandments and is not seen to be coming from

---

[25] Not a direct quotation. Isaiah 6:9
[26] Unknown reference.
[27] Matthew 7:6

worldly things, the only one of them to be found that does not spring from such things. But although we do not have demonstrations which reveal the Trinity, and other things which pertain to our faith (for faith did not at that time deserve a price), yet we have the power of the Gospel, to which the Koran also bears witness. Likewise we have miracles, while they have neither powers nor miracles.

For although about God the Koran says, "Do not say three Gods",[28] and immediately gives its reasoning saying that He is One. Yet we do not say anything contrary to this, but we also support this, in the places where it says that there is one God, whom we say is not only one, but most single. Nor do we attribute to Him any partner or likewise any sharer as they themselves do – namely the mind of the world, or the Word, or the Spirit or some divine intellect like a servant, more than enough according to our words. However, one should not reach for the divine majesty with human reasoning, nor suppose that it does not exist because these people cannot understand the discerning of the persons, despite which they also divide the essence. But they do not have such strong arguments for this that we cannot loosen. This, therefore, is enough for defending the faith.

From there, however, it is of more benefit to ask them what the Koran wants to say to them when it so often portrays God speaking about Himself in the plural, though He is simple and one. Moreover, this should be asked of them so that they are forced to acknowledge this number[29] amongst themselves.

However, concerning the mystery of the incarnation, which they themselves certainly deny in its entirety, but we believe, following the words of the gospels, we should enquire of them from where they know that it is impossible for God to have became incarnate. For it is either because He was not able (and this is false. For since He is omnipotent, all things are possible, in which there is no contradiction), or because He did

---

[28] K. 4.171

[29] Number: as in the grammatical term used for singular or plural.

not know how to do this (the same response as I said before), or He did not want to. And who was His advisor? Or was He indeed able to do it, just as He made the sun and moon which still exist, but did not do it? However, as one can see, it is impossible for them to show this, that He was not incarnate.

Concerning the divinity of Christ, however, Mohammed certainly uses this argument, that Christ never said that he himself was God. But although he did not say this openly about himself before the resurrection, yet he revealed this adequately saying: "I am that which I have been saying to you from the beginning."[30] And he commended Peter for what he said clearly, saying: "Blessed are you, Simon son of Jonah" and so on.[31] However, he himself did not want to say this conspicuously, because he came secretly, not with force, but with discretion and humility, to conquer him who conquered mankind with a trick. Therefore it was because of this plan that Christ did not before the resurrection say about himself: I am God. Following this reasoning, nor does a fisherman proclaim to the fish that, though there is food in the meal, there is a hook in the food. After the resurrection, however, he showed this clearly, giving out the Holy Spirit and the power to forgive sins, saying, "Receive the Holy Spirit, and whoever you forgive", and so on.[32] And Thomas also openly confessed it, saying this: "My Lord and my God!"[33] However, with this given, that nothing was said by Christ, because he certainly spoke with humility, but also revealed his ministry clearly, it is enough that His disciples say this clearly, who made signs like Christ did while they were saying this.

But since the Saracens deny the miracles and words of the apostles because they are contrary to the Koran, it must be insisted in the confutation of a law so deceitful, that it is not the law of God, and that the Saracens ought to accept the Gospel

---

[30] John 8:25
[31] Matthew 16:17
[32] John 20:22
[33] John 20:28

testimonies as well as those of the Old Testament. This, however, is possible to demonstrate through the Koran itself, with the result that Goliath will be killed by his own sword.

CHAPTER THREE. THAT THIS LAW IS NOT THE LAW OF GOD, BECAUSE NEITHER THE OLD NOR THE NEW TESTAMENT BEAR WITNESS TO IT. AND THAT IT IS NECESSARY FOR THE SARACENS TO OBEY THE WORDS OF THE OLD TESTAMENT AND GOSPEL.

Thirdly, it is also fitting to know that the Koran is not the law of God, for neither the Old Testament nor the Gospel bear witness to this, whereas the Koran testifies to both of these, because they are truly the laws of God. However, Mohammed alone instituted himself and presented a testimony from himself. For the law of God is like a chain, made continuous by the same author, and all of the links join each other, and all of the prophets prophesy about another and are mindful of this fact, and all of them prophesied about Christ. If, therefore, the law of the Saracens is also the law of God, and there is a calling to this law, not a perversion, but a conversion, as they themselves say, how is it that he remained unknown to the other prophets, so that no-one said anything about him? For we find nothing in Moses or in any other of the prophets or in Christ himself saying anything about Mohammed or about the law according to him, except when he says we should beware of false prophets.

However, Christ also said that the law and prophets up to John existed so that the world would recognise that no-one would come after this prophet, that no-one coming from anywhere would be a prophet in whom everyone should hope. However, Mohammed said that he himself was a prophet for everyone. Yet we do not know if he is a prophet at all. What we do know is that there has never been such a seducer in the world who has obtained so many men and peoples as followers for himself in so short a time.

Yet to this the Saracens respond that Moses and the other prophets had prophesied about Mohammed, but Christ prophesied about him more clearly by so much that he even mentioned his name, when he said to the sons of Israel, "I announce to you the apostle of God, who will come after me, and his name is Mohammed."[34] But the Jews corrupted the law of Moses and the prophets and the Christians corrupted the Gospel so that none of the truth remained in the law or gospels apart from what is in the Koran.

I will show that this is unworkable; firstly through the Koran. For it says in the chapter about Jonah, "If you are in doubt concerning what We have revealed to you, ask those who have read the Book before you."[35] However, those who read the Book before the Saracens were the Christians and Jews, who received the Pentateuch and the Gospel, as Mohammed himself sets out. That man, therefore, tells the Saracens to make enquiries from Christians and Jews concerning ambiguous matters. However, how is it that Mohammed sent these people back to false testimonies, if he really was a genuine prophet, as they say? Therefore at the time of Mohammed, the books of the Christians and Jews were not corrupt; neither is it possible to say that they were corrupted after this time. For it says in the chapter *Al-Hijr*, which means 'the stone', "We (it speaks as the character of God) revealed the warnings of God, and we will preserve the same."[36] However, the warnings are said among them to be the Gospel and the Law of Moses. God therefore

---

[34] K. 61.6
[35] K. 10.94
[36] K. 15.9

preserved the testimony of His own scripture among the faithful before Mohammed and He will preserve it after this age. Likewise in the chapter called *Al-Ma'idah*, which means 'the table', it says what judge Empacoene said to Mohammed when the Jews were approaching him for justice and judgement, "If they come to you , judge between them fairly. For God loves those who deal justly. But how will they come to you for judgement when they already have the Old Testament, in which there is the Justice of God?"[37]

Likewise, it is impossible that such great corruption and change was common and universal. For other peoples would also have been able to know if this were the case. But nor were there any hidden in particular places, for some books could have been able to be left untouched and without corruption[38] in this way, but the Law and Gospel are found written the same in every language and province. Likewise the four gospels were not published at the same time or in the same place nor in the same individual style by the same author. Indeed, Matthew wrote in Hebrew in Judaea, then John wrote in Greek in Asia, and Luke did so in the same language in Achaia, and Mark actually wrote in Latin in Italy. However, their meaning was put into Latin through the work of Jerome and others before the time of Mohammed, and copies continued in all languages. Therefore it is not possible that through any corruptions, the books were so useless that they were not known.

Likewise there is nothing in the faith so necessary and especially difficult, as the incarnation of the Word: that is, that that man is God. Concerning this, it was difficult to persuade the world. Whereby the Romans and other impious people persecuted Christians everywhere continually for three hundred years and refused to accept the Gospel or the faith, because they would not say that that man was God, not because they had never before then accepted both men and women as gods and goddesses, but because the Romans did not permit Christ to be

---

[37] K. 5.42-43

[38] i.e. the corruption the Christians and Jews allegedly inserted.

called God. They forbade it so that no god was honoured apart from the opinion of the Senate, because this God did not accept a partner. For if they accepted this, they would have been forced to give up their other gods, which was itself contrary to the customs of the provinces and of the Roman laws. How is it, therefore, that the Christians, to the loss of their very own men and in the destruction of their faith and to the provocation of the Roman leaders against them began to add to the gospels an element which is not persuasive? For everyone knows that this law is most holy and most rational, a law which most certainly includes the whole doctrine of this which I now say, namely, that man is most certainly God. Therefore, if it was fitting for the Christians to change any of those things which are in the Gospel, they would have changed them from the beginning, and they would have taken away anything that was not persuasive and added things which persuade, rather than the other way round.

Likewise, how on earth would the Christians have been able to come together with the Jews (who are divided by an age old hatred), as they were corrupting the scriptures and greatly adding to that in which they certainly do agree? For nor do the Jews say that Christ was God or a good man, from where the Christians agree more with the Saracens who say that Christ was a very holy man to a lesser extent.[39]

Likewise before the coming of Mohammed, the Christians, especially in the East, were divided into various sects, notably the Nestorians and the Jacobites. However, the Nestorians agree with the Saracens to the greatest extent, whereby Mohammed also ordered that they be especially honoured. Therefore in what way could the Jacobites have been able to come together with the Nestorians for corrupting the gospels, they who were divided by such a hatred between each other that they would even kill each other? However, I myself have looked at the Law

---

[39] The logic is that the Christians were more likely to co-operate with the Muslims than the Jews, and they would certainly never have co-operated with the Muslims, making co-operation with the Jews absolutely impossible.

and Gospel among them both and it is the same as it is among us.

Likewise, by whose influence would the Christians have removed the name Mohammed from the gospels when he gives so much praise to Christ and his mother and the Gospel? Whereby it says in the Koran that there is uprightness and perfection in the Gospel of Christ. And yet they did not remove from it instead the name of the devil, or Pilate who had Christ whipped, or at least the name of Judas, who betrayed him.

Likewise, whatever was the reason why Christians added to the Gospel that Christ was crucified and died, and was seen by men of good repute to have been crucified for certain, and disagreeing with this entirely, that he was God, as it says in the Gospel? However, they can have this line of reasoning; that these two things, though they differ so greatly, were founded in their own doctrines, just as the same man is clearly true God and truly died.

Likewise how is it that the Christians added this corruption to all the books in all places? For who could have persuaded everyone and fixed that corruption in their hearts? And yet the whole world was persuaded: it was so great that leaders, tyrants and philosophers accepted this from unlearned and poor men. Hence even the Caliph in Baghdad died a Christian, and a cross was found around his neck to testify that the very leader of the Saracens died a Christian. Whereby it is also shown that this Caliph was buried in a special way, apart from the rest and away from the place where it was the custom to bury others. And I myself saw this tomb in Baghdad. Therefore it makes sense in every way, by the testimony of the Koran, and by strong demonstrations and by clear proofs, that the Gospel is uncorrupted and unaltered.

Therefore, seeing that Mohammed praises the Gospel above other scriptures and after that the Old Testament, the Saracens could be compelled to accept the words contained in the gospels and the Old Testament most conformably. Likewise in the chapter *Al-Ma'idah*, which means 'table', it says that the people of the book are nothing unless they fulfil the Law and

Gospel. Moreover, it says that the Saracens are the people of the book, whereby it says, "Unless they fulfil the Law and Gospel, and similarly with that which was revealed to you" (that is, the Koran, which they believe was revealed to the Saracens). Therefore it is necessary for them also to have the law and Gospel just as they have the Koran, and to preserve it to this day. However, the fact that the Saracens are called the people of the book, in agreement with what Mohammed meant, is shown in many places in the Koran. For it says in the chapter *An-Nisa'* (which translates as 'women'), near the end, that the Saracens should not waver in this law. Whereby it is written, "O people of the Book, refuse to waver in your law and do not talk about God beyond the truth."[40] These things which are in that chapter show that the people of the book are called Saracens. Moreover, this is also shown clearly in the chapter *Tulem*,[41] near the end of the book.

However, if they argue and want to say that the Gospel and Old Testament are completely corrupt, let them show the unchanged version of that which has been changed, and we will accept that. Moreover let them especially show one version in every language, as we have shown them. It is clear, therefore, that the Koran is not the law of God because neither the Old Testament nor the Gospel, which are divine laws, and which Mohammed confesses, bear witness to it, but rather, they oppose it.

---

[40] K. 4.171
[41] Unknown reference.

CHAPTER FOUR. THAT THE KORAN IS NOT THE LAW OF GOD, BECAUSE IT DOES NOT HAVE A STYLE OR IDIOM WHICH AGREES WITH OTHERS.

Fourthly, it is fitting to know that the Koran is not the law of God, because it does not have the same style or idiom as that of the divine law. And so it is rhythmical in style or metrical and full of flattery and fictitious in its stories. However, the fact that it is rhythmical in style is clear through the whole book to those reading it. However, I cannot set out an example of this, because it is not possible for the rhythm or verse to be properly preserved in every way when it is translated into Latin.

However, the Saracens in Arabia especially exult in this fact, that the reciting of the law which is among them has grandeur and rhythm, and that particularly in this way it is shown that the book has been composed by God and that it was revealed to Mohammed, according to the reciting. Since Mohammed was illiterate, he did not know such a way of thinking and way of speaking.[42] The antithesis to this is clear. For we see in the divine scriptures God speaking with Moses and other prophets, but never talking to them in rhythm or verse. Moreover, Mohammed says that the law of Moses and the Gospel are from God, that God gave the books to Moses and to Christ. But these are not metrical or rhythmical. And none of the other prophets who heard God's voice said that God spoke in metre - a view that both wise men and philosophers despise.

---

[42] K. 7.160, "So believe in Allah and His Messenger, the unlettered Prophet".

Whereby certain people even brought this to Mohammed, as it says in the chapter *Al-Anbiya'*, which means 'prophets', saying to him, "So you are certainly more of a dreamer; certainly more a dancer",[43] and they accused him of other things such as these, thinking that this reciting was not only not from God, but not even altogether prophetic.

However, in addition, this law is full of flattery in its words, and more than anyone could believe or say. For at any time throughout the whole book, he has woven beneath it nothing worthy of praise, but only that God is great and glorious and wise and good, and that everything is His that is in the sky and on the earth and everything which is in between, and that He judges fairly. And following whatever word he repeats a hundred times and more, after this, he also says: there is no God but God, trust in God and in his apostle, calling himself the apostle of God. And he says that all these words were from the very mouth of God, without a mediator, also insofar as Mohammed did not know how to say these things. But this is not the custom for God, that He speaks about Himself as if speaking about another, that God is great and glorious and other things of this kind, which he is accustomed to repeat.

This must also be noted, that this law makes use of most disgraceful names, especially carnal ones, such as these, namely, sex and extravagance, as is the custom for those whose attention is turned to the earth. Now concerning the way of speaking and thinking, it is sure and clear to all who read it, that it is fictitious. But although this is the case throughout, yet I will point out a few things which seem worthy of praise in some places. For it says in the chapter *An-Naml*, which means 'ant', that Solomon assembled a large army of angels and men and irrational animals. However, as they were moving away, they came to something like a river of ants, and then he now said to an ant, "O ant, get yourselves into your homes, in case Solomon and his army destroys you." And the ant smiled. And a little later, all the birds were found in the army, but the ant was not there.

---

[43] K. 21.5

And Solomon said, "Why is it that I do not see the ant? I will punish her, and cut off her head, if she does not give me a reason why she is not here, but a long way off." And she said, "I have learned what you do not know, and I have come to you from Sheba with true tidings. For I found a woman ruling over them, and I learned that she and her people worship the sun apart from God," and the rest.[44]

Likewise in the chapter *Al-Qamar*, which means 'moon', it says, "The hour has approached, and the moon is destroyed."[45] Scholars interpreting this say that Mohammed stood with his friends. However, seeing the moon coming near to its zenith, they said to him: Show us some portent.[46] And then with his two fingers, he indicated at the moon, that is, with his thumb and middle finger. When he had done this, the moon was split into two parts and indeed, one part fell onto mount Clibais, which hangs over a part of Mecca, while the other part went to the other mountain which is called Rubus, situated at another part of the city. However, the moon, divided in such a way, went into the tunic of Mohammed, and he himself repeated this again.

Likewise, in the chapter *Saba'* it says that a worm showed Solomon's death to demons. Here the narration says that Solomon, supported by his staff, was suddenly seized by such grief that he immediately died; but by some divine miracle he did not fall. However, the demons who were serving him, seeing that he was standing, believed that he was sleeping. And indeed, worms were born out of the ground and chewed up the staff on which he was leaning. After this was consumed, Solomon fell. And then the demons, moving swiftly, realised that he was dead, and because of that, they began to be able to hurt men nearby.[47]

---

[44] K. 27.17-24
[45] K. 54.1
[46] *Sahih Al-Bukhari* Vol. 4 Hadith No. 831, "Narrated Anas that the Meccan people requested Allah's apostle to show them a miracle, and so he showed them the splitting of the moon."
[47] K. 34.14

Likewise in the chapter *The Story*, Mohammed himself gives the reason why wine is prohibited. For he says that God sent two angels to earth in order to give good orders and to judge fairly. And these angels were Harut and Marut.[48] However, a certain woman, coming to them, having justice, invited them to lunch and put wine before them, wine that God had commanded them not to drink. However, when they were intoxicated, they demanded that she sleep with them. She agreed, but stipulated beyond this, however, that one of them should indeed make her go up into heaven, and the other make her truly descend. And she went up into heaven. However, God, seeing her and hearing the justice which she had, made her a bearer of light, so that she was just as beautiful among the stars in heaven as she also was among women on earth. However, when the choice was given to the sinning angels when they wanted to be punished, evidently now or in the future, since they chose rather to be punished in the present, he made them hang by their feet by an unyielding chain in a Babylonian well until the day of judgement.

These and ones like these are contained in the before mentioned law, because of which any sort of man who is wise can certainly realise the fact that the law is not divine in any way, for God is not accustomed to speaking with men though fictitious tales.

---

[48] Mentioned in K. 2.102

CHAPTER FIVE. THAT THE KORAN IS NOT THE LAW OF GOD, SINCE IT DOES NOT AGREE IN ITS OPINIONS WITH ANYONE ELSE.

It is also clear for the following reason that the Koran is not the law of God, because of the fact that it does not agree with the law of God, nor with philosophers, who discussed virtues and the final end that is in store for men. For philosophers supposed that happiness itself was, for man, in the intellectual part of the soul, and that the greatest intellect in man is a power which exists only for the extremely intelligent. And that happiness is the reward for virtue, and that virtue is about great and difficult things and other things of such a kind, though they could not understand such things perfectly.

However, Christ showed these very things in the Gospel, saying that the path is narrow which leads to eternal life, and few are they who arrive through it, but the path is wide which leads to destruction, [49] and the rest. However, in this he agrees with Aristotle's opinion, who says that it is a difficult thing to live according to virtue, just as it is to find the centre of a circle, which few people can do.[50]

Likewise, however, Christ also put the happiness of man in the observance of God, saying, "And this is life eternal, that they might know thee the only true God."[51] However, these very things are very well known because of the Old Testament. For promises were made to Abraham, to whom God especially

---

[49] Matthew 7:13-14
[50] centre of a circle: Aristotle, *Nicomachean Ethics*, Book II.9
[51] John 17:3

promised that He Himself would put him in the Promised Land and give him the blessing of descendants.   And moreover, Moses, to whom God granted so many extraordinary favours, who also saw God in a cloud, thinking that this was not enough for him, constantly sought to see the face of God and His glory.[52]

However, Mohammed hardly discussed anything about virtues, but about war and plunder. He chose the wide path conveniently for himself and for his own followers, sons of destruction and death.   Whereby to their own detriment, it profits them to say, "There is no God but God, and Mohammed is the apostle of God." However, about the final end, he agrees with none except certain ancients, who lived an irrational life, and who make no distinction between intellect and sense. Whereby they also claim that heavenly happiness lies in certain sensations, namely, in foods and intemperance, and in gardens and expensive clothes. We will make observations about these things later in the sixth chapter.

And it is not possible for them to say these things definitively, as if there is also mention in the Gospel of a table and food and of such things in heaven. However, these things are shown definitively according to the Gospel, since many things are also openly said in it about eternal blessedness. But in the Koran, nothing whatsoever is clearly said about true blessedness, but just as it agrees with the man who understands nothing of this, yet only according to the writing, it portrays heavenly happiness as concordant with the sort of thing that the carnal and intemperate man desires.

But although he neither considers nor promises anything about true happiness for men, yet he did demonstrate certain truths and signs concerning the final end of the Saracens, as if inspired by the Holy Spirit. For Mohammed himself said to the Saracens: After me you will be divided into seventy three parts of which one will be saved. Truly all the rest will be destroyed in the fire. This belief is so strong among them that no-one, wise of lacking wisdom, despises it.

---

[52] ...to see the face of God and His glory: for example, Exodus 33:13-20.

However, another similar belief about that is in the Koran in the chapter *Mariam*, which means 'Mary', which says that all the Saracens will go to hell.[53] This belief I trust to be most true, though it was before delivered by the mouth of a liar on his death-bed. And in this the false prophet agrees with the first truth, which says: Wide is the path which leads to destruction and many are they who pass through it. Therefore it clearly corresponds, after the above words, that the law of the Saracens is wide-spread, and there are many Saracens who pass through it and go across into the fire. And this is clear not only according to the voice of truth, but according to the voice of the prophet who is among them.

Likewise, the Koran does not agree with the law of Moses in the commandments, and it turns us away in these things. For the law of God forbids murder, rape, and all worldly desires. However, the Koran either orders them or permits them to happen. Likewise, it does not agree with the Jews. For the Law of Moses and the Gospel say that no-one ought to be condemned by one witness, but that every word stands on the account of two or three witnesses.[54] Contrary statements to these, however, are found in the chapter *An-Nur*, which means 'light', where it prohibits them from compelling women to let go of their virginity, but tells them they can sleep safely with those who are consenting.[55] However, this itself is also clear in the chapter *Al-Mu'minun*, where it permits them to mix with their own wives as well as with those which they can capture in war.[56] Therefore it is clear that the law of the Koran is not the law of God, nor is it from God (except in the sense of with His permission, just as other things are), for it differs in its purpose from the law of God, who desires the salvation of men.

---

[53] K. 19.71

[54] Deuteronomy 17:6 and 19:15 (2 Corinthians 13:1). Matthew 18:16. 1 Timothy 5:19. Hebrews 10:28.

[55] K. 24.33

[56] K. 23.6

CHAPTER SIX. THAT THE KORAN IS NOT THE LAW OF GOD, SINCE IT CONTRADICTS ITSELF IN MANY PLACES.

Sixthly, it should be observed that the law of the Koran is not only denied by divine law, but even disagrees with itself here and there, because it is evil. And Mohammed himself shows this. For it says in the chapter *An-Nisa'*, which means 'women', "If this Koran did not come from God, many contrasts and contradictions would have been found in it."[57]

For he himself says in many places, that God does not direct the wanderer; and yet in many places he himself seems to beg that they be directed from the darkness into the light and out of unrighteousness into righteousness. Likewise, he says about himself that he was made an orphan in sin, for he was an idolater. But moreover, he himself says that God made him such a prophet, since, when God sent for him, he ascended to God and to the seventh heaven. And he was granted a favour by a certain angel who was a thousand times greater than the world, whom he found mourning for his sins.

Likewise, he says that he is a prophet for all people; yet he says that the Koran was given by God in Arabic letters and that no other language can know him but Arabic.

Likewise, he says in the chapter *Al-Baqarah*, which means 'cow', that the Jews and Christians and Sabians will be saved.[58]

---

[57] K. 4.82
[58] K. 2.62

And after these things, in the chapter *Al 'Imran* he says that no-one will be saved but those who live by the law of the Saracens.[59]

Also, he himself commands these people not to argue with men of another sect with course words, but with pleasant ones. For it is not for man to bring down, but for God alone. And the One Unknowable will pay back the reckoning for himself alone, not for anyone else. However, after this, he himself commands in many places that everyone be killed and plundered who does not believe, unless they believe or pay a tribute.[60] Likewise he himself says in the chapter *Consultation*, that of those who accept another God other than God, you should not be their protector or guardian, but God has kept this for Himself alone.[61] Yet this contradiction is worthy of praise; here he certainly commanded so often that the infidels be killed, but there he commands the opposite, that no-one be the punisher of such wickedness, but the punishment for these people is saved for God alone.

Likewise, he himself, in the chapter *Al-Baqarah*, in the end, discusses himself, saying that he is not one of those who compel others to believe.[62] But how is this true? Since he himself commands those who do not believe to be killed and plundered, for what greater compulsion is there than slaughter?

Likewise, in the chapter of the cow, he concedes that it is not unnatural for men and women to be mixed. For he tells the Saracens not to defile themselves with the infidels before they believe.[63] And about women, he says, "Your women are your land; plough them as you will."[64] But yet earlier in the same chapter, he said that the Sodomites at the time of Lot had committed a detestable sin, one which was also the custom for nations which had existed before.

---

[59] K. 3.19
[60] K. 9.29
[61] *Ash-Shura* K. 42.47
[62] K. 2.256
[63] K. 2.221
[64] K. 2.223

Likewise, he himself says about Abraham, Isaac and Jacob and his sons, that they were Saracens.[65] But yet, he himself says that it was revealed to him by God, that he is clearly the first Saracen in this faith. Therefore, how were those men Saracens, if Mohammed was the first of all the Saracens? Likewise, it was not necessary for people to be Saracens before the wide-spread law of the Saracens existed. Moreover, the law of the Saracens is the Koran, which now exists and was given after the Law of Moses and the Gospel, just as it says in the Koran itself. It was not much more than seven hundred years ago that Mohammed lived. For he began in the five hundred and ninety eighth year after the nativity of our Lord. However, Noah and Abraham and Isaac and Jacob lived before the Gospel and before Moses. However, if he says that these men are Saracens because they got to know what the things of the law were, then indeed, they would have been able to be Saracens in every respect which they got to know since they were prophets. However, if they say that the Koran is pleasing to them, this is also impossible. For they did the contrary to many things that are ordained by the Koran.

Likewise, he himself says that prophesying is forbidden, and yet he himself says after this in the chapter *Elaphar*, "Let us prophesy, if otherwise you are unable, in the cleft of the finger. And whoever does not do this, let him be condemned."

Likewise, he himself says that he was sent by God to the Arabs, because these people do not have any apostle from God. Moreover, he also says that the Koran was given in the Arabic language alone, and he also says that he does not know any language but Arabic. Whereby though a certain Jacobite Mapyra had clung to Mohammed, and Salonus the Persian, and Abdullah from Persia, and Selbeam the Jew, and then some others said that they were instructing him, he even fell on to his face, and his hands and feet were together, and his friends completely covered him with their clothes. And finally coming back to his senses, he said, "God sent me to rebuke you for the speech that you have said, which such people teach me." And

---

[65] K. 2.133

he read to them one sentence, which is at the end of the passage *An-Nahl*, which means 'palm', which says this, "We know what they themselves say, that they instruct him when they speak thus to him in the Persian language; this, however, is in eloquent Arabic."[66] He also says after this, "How can they teach me, they of whom one is certainly Persian, another actually Hebrew?" These men said to him, "We can speak with you and relate to you in our own languages, moreover, we can instruct you in every way in your own language." He found no response to this. But if he was not able to be instructed by a Hebrew and a Persian, which are close, how was he able to teach people who are more removed from his language? However, after this, he himself says that he was sent to the entirety of peoples.[67] But how was he able to come to all peoples who were divided into seventy languages, he who did not know how to explain his message in any language other than Arabic?

Therefore the contradiction is clear, and the lie is clear, that the same man was sent to the Arabs alone, and to every people. Therefore it is not the law of God, in which one can find so many contradictions.

---

[66] K. 16.103
[67] K. 21.106-107 and K. 6.90

CHAPTER SEVEN. THAT THE LAW OF THE SARACENS IS NOT CONFIRMED BY ANY MIRACLE.

Seventh, it must be considered that the Koran is not a law of God which is confirmed by miracles, nor is Mohammed the apostle of God; for no miracle bears witness to this. For when God sent Moses to Pharaoh, He showed great portents, and then Elijah and Elisha and other prophets similarly performed great and unheard of miracles, and especially those who were bringing something new into the way of life. Moreover, Christ particularly came in the greatest miracles and signs, just as Mohammed himself also says in the Koran.[68]

However, if the Saracens say that Mohammed performed many great miracles, such as renewing again the split moon, and the spring of water flowing from the midst of his fingers, it is a fabrication and contrary to the same Koran. For Mohammed forbids accepting any such thing about him beyond the things which are written in the Koran. About all the prophets he says, "Many have invented many things; what some do not suppose about me, that alone is the truth which should be believed about me, which is supported by the authority of the Koran." For since that man did not do miracles, and he wanted to explain this, he presents God speaking and explaining, "The Lord said to me: Because of this do I not permit you to do miracles, lest on account of the miracles there come about for you what also happened to the other prophets." Therefore he is convicted by his own testimony that he did no sign. For Mohammed himself says continually in the Koran that, when men say to him, "Show some sign just as Moses, and others, clearly, came with signs,

---

[68] K. 3.49

and just as Christ and the other prophets did", he responds, "Because Moses and the prophets were sent by God, and especially Christ,[69] who came in the greatest portents, and the world did not believe these people, but it said that these men were sorcerers and magicians. Because of this, God did not permit me to perform miracles - for they would not have believed - but I came in the power of arms."

However, in this it is shown most clearly that it is false. For how would they not have believed him doing miracles, who without miracles trusted the baseness of the command to kill and to plunder and to ravage many women, and gouge out tooth for tooth and eye for eye? For they who live in the world are inclined towards such things, whereby they can hardly be restrained by many judges, torturers and punishments.

However, because he takes charge in the power of arms instead of a miracle, the lie is clear. For he was not always the victor, as Moses and Joshua son of Nun and Elijah were, whom the angel of the Lord always protected and made victorious. However, Mohammed conquered sometimes, and at other times was conquered, just like other tyrants. For his appearance was battered and his teeth ground in war. From this it is clear that it is no miracle, which is seized on by them as a sign, that a large part of the world suddenly clung to him, as one can see. For he set up such a law, and gave such commands of the sort to which men were inclined without laws, as is clear to higher beings. "For the Lord commanded me", he said, "to conquer peoples by the sword until the time they confess that there is no God but God, and that I am the apostle of God."

Those who had confessed this, they kept their money safe from him as well as their blood. From this also the Saracens are called saved. For those who accepted the commands of Mohammed were saved from him and from those who were under him, and they did not kill them or plunder them. From where the Saracens are not called Saracens, but *Muslims*, which means 'saved'. And they mock Christians who say that they

---

[69] K. 3.45

themselves are saved. Moreover, while many people were accepting such safety from Mohammed for the above mentioned reason, after this, he ordered it to be proclaimed that whoever says "There is no God but God", he will enter into paradise, even if he is an adulterer or a plunderer. However, a certain man called Abu Darr came to him asking whether this was true, and he replied, "Certainly." But he added to the above words, "Even if he drinks wine, or even murders?" And Mohammed added, "Even then, if he twists his nostrils." However, to confirm all these things, he shows no sign, but bares the sword.

The same thing is contained in the chapter of the prophets, for there it reads like this, They said concerning Mohammed, "That is something you heard in a dream, you compose blasphemies, or you sing strongly: come to us with one miracle, like the ones that were sent before." He responded, "God said, we destroyed cities for the people who did not believe, and after this, those who were before you did not believe. But nor do you believe unless by the sword."

Moreover, he would claim that Gabriel was sent to him by God, bringing to him some kind of animal, more than an ass, yet less than a mule, but the animal's name was Alborach. Moreover, the animal had been speaking and walking a path for fifty thousand years to the hour, and it had been doing this in the night. And certain other fables which will be discussed after this in the tenth chapter.

However, the Christian faith, which teaches difficult things, was wholly founded on clear, meaningful miracles, which not only Christ performed, but also his disciples after him, as well as teachers who put forth the Gospel and the writings of the apostles. And they continue the miracles even up to the present time: of demons, whom they cast out; of the cripples, whom they cure; and of the dead, whom they raise to life. However, Christians have done and are doing these miracles, saying that the crucified Christ is the only true God.

If the Saracens say they do not believe these things, as if these things were not done, let me show them a greater miracle. For it is clear that before Christ, almost the whole world was paying homage to idols, but especially the Romans, who held a monopoly of power over the world. But these people accepted the faith of the Christians and not only believed the crucified Christ to be true God, but also rejected all the other Gods, who for such a great time had given them their answers through idolatry, and moreover, imposed nothing burdensome, though the Christian faith had imposed difficult things on the world, since it was thus accustomed. Difficult things such as to hate the world, to hate oneself, to love one's enemies, to pray for one's persecutors, to bless one's wrongdoers, not to plunder another's property, but to give away one's own. The world accepted all of this, throwing away its former ceremony. Therefore either it was persuaded with an adequate number of miracles, or with no miracles. However, it is an even greater miracle that this was also able to happen without miracles, through uneducated and simple men. And the Christians did this not killing others, but patiently enduring the death brought to them by others.

Therefore it is clear in every way that the faith of Christians was founded on baffling miracles, but moreover, that the faith of Mohammed is founded on no miracle. For the above description is what a faith is like which does not lack miracles, but especially according to the Saracens, those carnal and worldly men. And yet the more sensible of these, who have the skill of letter writing and claim honour for themselves by strength, hold to no faith in this.

CHAPTER EIGHT. THAT THE LAW OF MOHAMMED IS IRRATIONAL.

Eighth, it must be considered that even without any miracles, it would have been possible for the law of Mohammed to be accepted by the world and declared just like the law of God is, so long as it was rational. It is, however, completely irrational; because of the man who brought the law, because of the law itself, because of the works and because of the end.[70]

Firstly, therefore, it is most clear that it is irrational because of the law-giver. So it is entirely irrational that such a holy law (as they themselves claim, namely, that the Koran is the Word of God) was given by such an unjust man, a plunderer, an adulterer, a murderer and a man submissive to other sins, that are all clear to those who know about his life. But the Saracens reply to this, that David also fell into adultery and bloodshed at the same time;[71] moreover, Moses[72] was a murderer. Thus it is also possible to say about Mohammed that he was the true prophet of God, even though he was sometimes in the power of sin. Indeed, regardless of such things, he was a genuine prophet of God. But this holds no strength at all. For David and Moses set right their own sin with repentance, and this is evident. For David announced his own sin and he caused himself deep grief, whereby he also gained pardon. From there, after he said, "I have sinned," Nathan said to him from the mouth of God, "The Lord forgives you your sin."[73] However, about Mohammed, it is

---

[70] The end, i.e. life after death.
[71] 2 Samuel 11
[72] Exodus 2:12
[73] 2 Samuel 12:13

by no means said that he either announced his sin or repented. Indeed, he rather then added blasphemy, asserting it as true by an unjust law.[74]

For as it is well known by all Saracens, Mohammed was strongly in love with a certain girl called Mary, as she was called by the Jacobites, a girl whom Macobeus the king of the Jacobites gave to him. However, two of Mohammed's wives, one called Aisha - the daughter of Abu Bakr, the most noble of the rest - the other Hafsa, the daughter of Omar, became jealous of Mary. One day, these two came to him and found him as he was sleeping with Mary, and they said, "Is this fitting for a prophet to do?" He was embarrassed and vowed that he would never after this sleep with Mary. And so the two were pleased with his oath. However, after a little time had passed, he was not able to restrain himself. Wherefore he brought the law even as if it were from the mouth of God, who revealed to him and brought an opinion into the Koran, in the chapter *At-Tahrim*, which means 'prohibition', or 'anathema', where it says, "O prophet, do you forbid that which God has permitted you? You seek to be gratified by your wives. Now God has brought you the law, so that you may release your oaths."[75] In this way, he swore falsely and slept with her again, saying that God had released the oath for him, and in addition to this, Michael and Gabriel were witnesses. And one of his wives said to him, "O Mohammed, God is very eager in [aiding] your licentiousness."[76] Then because of this, he wanted to say, "Perhaps God is jealous for you, since he shares with you this hostile task." And he added, "Surely God Himself did not command you to do this, since you bear witness to this by your speech? Perhaps God seeks to show kindness to you and approach you." However, he himself read to his two wives together what follows in the chapter *Prohibition* and he said it as if it came from God's person, "You should

---

[74] The blasphemy: lies, intended to legitimate his sins, pretended to be from the mouth of God.

[75] K. 66.1-2

[76] *Sahih Al-Bukhari* Vol.6, 311. The words of Mohammed's wife Aisha. This was also in response to the revelation K. 33.51.

repent before God, since your hearts have turned away,"[77] talking about the accusation by which they accused him of incest. And then it follows, "If by chance he[78] divorces you, I God will give him in your place wives better than you, Saracens, faithful, wealthy, penitent and devout, alert minded and still maidens." When they heard this, they said, "We repent."

However, he did the same thing again when he took the wife of Zaid. For he said the phrase in the chapter *Al-Ahzab*, that God said, "You rival in your heart with what God has made manifest, and you fear men. But it is more right to fear God."[79] For when Zaid had divorced her, he said, "Apostle of God, you should not take her as your wife." And Mohammed replied, "Alas for you, God has given her to me." After this, he gave this news about himself, saying that God has given her to the prophet. See how he concealed a lesser sin with a greater one. And indeed, Mohammed himself says, "There is no sin greater than to attach a lie to God."[80] Likewise, there is no sin among prophets that is as insufferable as the combination of intemperance and lust, since the Holy Spirit does not touch the hearts of prophets in erotic activities, as Jerome says.[81] And the philosopher also says that mankind cannot be observed in such actions.[82]

It is, therefore, completely irrational that the minister and prophet of such a wholesome law (as they claim it to be) is a most carnal and lustful man. He himself boasts concerning himself, saying that he had as much strength in going on, and as much abundance of intemperance as forty men, though God deprived him of a progeny of sons, for it is said he only had one daughter. Therefore this law is irrational because of the law-

---

[77] K. 66.4-5

[78] he: Mohammed

[79] K. 33.37

[80] K. 18.15

[81] *Hieronymi Dialogus contra Luciferanios, cap. 9*: Spiritus quippe sanctus nisi mundam sedem non incolit.

[82] mankind: In other words, the humane and decent, thoughtful and rational side of man, in which moral superiority is supposed to exist.

bearer. Then because he is wicked and carnal; then because he is ignorant and unsure, as he even bears witness to in the Koran itself, that he does not know what will be for him or the Saracens, that he does not know whether he or they are on the path to salvation or not.

Neither is this law of itself in possession of reasoning, since it contains the most indecent names, and with regard to these, it should be covered up, especially with regard to the bodily and lustful ones. For in many places he uses this most indecent word, 'sex', which no other law does. Comic poets themselves scarcely use this word, poets for whom the substance of poetry is worldly and indecent, even if they do, rarely, just as Aratus shamelessly said, "I was not afraid while I had sex."

However, he himself also says this openly, "There is no man in the world who can understand the Koran." Yet how is it that God commanded it to be preserved, if he did not also give it to be understood? Moreover, it is fitting to know that there is nothing in the Gospel that we cannot also understand when aided by the lamp of faith.

But nor is it made rational by the doctrine contained in it. For it says in many places that God commanded the angels to worship Adam. Indeed, it says that those who refused became demons, but those who worshipped remained angels. Yet how is it that God would have commanded idol worship, and commanded that they give others the honour that is owed to God alone?

Likewise, also in the reasoning of doctrine, it is irrational because of their own words. For in that law, this is of the utmost necessity, that they say, as is said everywhere, that there is no God but God and Mohammed is the apostle of God, and in addition, that God is great. But what declaration is that?[83] For no one who can reason could say that God is small. Likewise, the statement that says, "There is no God but God" is true on its

---

[83] What... declaration: In other words, what makes this declaration *maxime necessarium*? (Because none of the three parts of the declaration are worth anything.)

own and no one contradicts this, whether God is one or several.[84] And in every instance, such duplication is most true. For there are no angels but angels, and there is no man but man, and there is no donkey but donkey; for a cow or a dog is not a donkey. However, where it says, "Mohammed is the apostle of God", this is strongly doubtful. What, therefore, is the reasoning for joining these two statements - the one well known and the other obscure? What virtue or what use is it, when whoever confesses this is automatically saved?

Likewise, Mohammed says in the aforementioned law, that all men were one, undivided, and belonging to one religion.[85] But God made them divided by sending various prophets. However, as far as it appears, this cannot be true. For the one God who especially loves unity also loves the safety of men. For he would not have divided men into various divisions, errors and destructions. But this was done by the hatred of the devil and the wickedness of man, though with the permission of God, who allows those who do not want to believe the truth to walk on in their diverse errors.

Likewise, in the aforementioned law, Mohammed orders, as if from the mouth of God, that the faithful be killed, that is, those who are not Saracens. Likewise, he says about them that they are not able to think rightly, since they are not led by God and God does not guide them.[86] But it would not work for them to be killed, because they cannot. But for those who they can kill, it is not fitting to compel them to work, since forced slavery is not pleasing to God. Yet Mohammed himself commands them to be killed unless they believe, or to be compelled to believe in some other way, and irrationally does he make this unsuitable judgement. For it says in the chapter 'Jonah', "If God had wanted, all would have believed who are now on the earth, and you would compel men to believe. No one can even have faith

---

[84] In other words, Trinitarians also believe this.
[85] K. 2.213
[86] K. 7.178

unless this is permitted him by God."[87]   However, we shall explain this at greater length later on in the ninth chapter.

However, this law is also irrational because of the things it discusses. For it has a separate chapter about an ant, and another about a spider, and another about smoke. But for who's sake did God command such things about the ant and smoke?

Likewise, he says that God could never spare someone who turned his back on the enemy,[88] and the rest. But what sin is it for a man to flee in war when he sees that he is in danger? Mohammed only wanted to make his men war-like and bold.

Likewise the law which he orders concerning washing, is completely irrational. For he commands them, when they wish to pray, to wash[89] their hands and face and bottom and forehead and the palms of the feet and the arms up to the elbow. However, if they cannot find water, he commands them to plunge their hands in the dust, and then rubbing the dust-smeared hands through the face, to adequately smear their own faces with the dust. But even though it is rational to wash, it would actually have been more rational to wash the soul, as Jeremiah says, "Cleanse your soul from wickedness."[90] However, to put dust on one's face, what reasoning can this have? Then indeed, as much as it is rational to wash, so much more is it unsatisfactory and irrational to be smeared with dust.

However, this law seems to be especially irrational when it describes divorce. For it is possible for a Saracen to throw out his wife and reconcile with her again as often as he is pleased or displeased with her. However, he cannot accept her again like this after the third divorce, unless someone else has known her sensually while she was not in her menstrual period. However, if no one else has known her sufficiently with an erect penis, it is further necessary for him to know her fully in this way. And so when they want to reconcile with their wives, they give her to

---

[87] K.10.99-100

[88] Referring to turning one's back in flight. K.8.15-16

[89] K. 5.6

[90] Jeremiah 4:14

someone obscure or some other worthless character, who is to sleep with her as his wife. And after this, he will testify publicly and say that he wishes to divorce her. After this is done, the first man may take her back to himself. However, when the second men are pleased with them so much that they do not want to be separated from them, then the first man grants his request and no longer hopes for his wife. However, the law for these things is not fitting for men so mush as for animals deprived of reason, and it is not consistent with God, who guides all creatures with reasoning.

However, this law is especially irrational because of what it says of the end[91] and the rewards which it promises. For it says throughout the Koran; the blessedness reserved for Saracens is to inherit watered gardens, women and mistresses, young, modest and beautiful, clothed in purple garments. Also to have golden and silver bowls place on tables scattered hare and there, and to have most pleasant food. He numbers those things at greatest length in the chapter *Ar-Rahman*, which means 'the compassionate'.[92] At any rate, in the book of Mohammed's doctrine, which is a book they have by a great author, it sets out the order of foods. Indeed, he says that the first dish of those which are placed before them there is liver with Albebuch fish, the most pleasant of foods. And after this comes the fruit of trees. And following in the same chapter, when some people asked him if they would live in luxury, he replied, "There would not be blessedness if any pleasure were not present there. Indeed, everything would be somewhat pointless if luxurious pleasure did not follow." However, herein lies the intention of the whole Koran and of the whole Saracen religion, to firmly place blessedness in luxury and in the belly. And he does not say these things as a parable or an example as the sacred scriptures also mention food and a table in the blessed life.[93]

---

[91] The end refers to eternal life.
[92] K. Surah 55
[93] Blessed life: heaven.

However, about true blessedness, such as about the speculation of God, or about the perfection of the mind, Mohammed makes no mention at all, because he does not eagerly desire this, nor does he cling to it. For the only things that he eagerly desires are what he also now promises. For in this he openly reveals himself to be contrary to Christ, and to all prophets and philosophers, and everyone who makes use of reason, who all jointly agree that the greatest blessedness for men lies in knowing God, just as in the Gospel according to John, "This is eternal life, that they know you, the only true God."[94] And Aristotle says that the life with intellect is the best kind. Then the life centred on the belly and the bed is the worst kind, because it would become an impediment to the moral excellence of intellect. But since the Saracens do not accept things said by the Holy Scriptures, nor by philosophers, because of the reasons mentioned previously in the first chapter,[95] we should now return to some reason, to which even those irrational people cannot completely say no.

And so let reason be our authority, without which no authority has strength. Let it also be shown that neither in the belly nor in intemperate actions does blessedness for men exist, and that these things will not be there. For everyone knows that we take food for this, so that the corruption which can occur may be avoided by means of the consumption of the natural fruit of the ground and so that there would be an increase.[96] However, these two things will not be there. For everyone will rise up equally both immortal and whole. Therefore the consumption of food is not at all necessary.

Yet similarly nor is the use of sexual activities, since it is not even necessary now, except in order to preserve the species, which cannot be preserved by someone on their own.

---

[94] John 17:3

[95] (As written above) "...he ordered that nothing whatsoever was worthy of trust that was contrary to the extensive law given by him, and meanwhile, he ordered that anyone who dared to say something contrary to this be punished with quite a severe penalty."

[96] Corruption: physical deterioration. Increase: growth in the body's physical strength and stature.

Likewise, men who will rise again, or will live forever, will also always be feeding.[97] And if they will always be feeding, it follows that their bodies will always grow. Actually, there will also be excretions there, and other foul things, since the same things would be turned out as were digested in the food. Both of these are unsatisfactory. To this, however, Mohammed responds in the book of his own doctrine, saying that there will be no excretion of filth there, but a purification through sweat. And he introduces the example of a boy in his mother's womb, who, as he says, is fed and does not excrete. But if one looks again closely at its solution, neither the example nor the reasoning of this [doctrine] is sufficient. For even the things which are perfect in an imperfect world would have been great imperfections in a perfect one.

Likewise, if there is to be the use of sexual activities there, unless they are in vain,[98] it would also follow that there will be procreation just as there is now. Therefore many people will be born after the resurrection who had not lived before the resurrection. Therefore, in vain has the resurrection of the dead been prolonged for so long so that everyone of the same state of being would be given life at the same time.[99]

Likewise, if blessedness lies in indulging oneself and in having many women who will be born after the resurrection, they will not be able to be blessed unless they take many women. However, they will not be able to take either the fortunate or the unfortunate, therefore they wait until more other women are born. And it will be necessary in this way for more women to be born, but few men. And so in a short time there will be an empire of women.

Likewise, if after the resurrection there will be the reproduction of men who will be born, either they will be

---

[97] If we follow the reasoning that there will be food in heaven.

[98] In vain: not producing any children.

[99] The reasoning is that the day of resurrection is the time when all humans, dead or living, receive their everlasting body all at the same time. The day of resurrection is prolonged for this reason. Therefore, procreation after the resurrection means that not all receive their bodies at the same time, upsetting the very reason for prolonging that day.

perishable again, or they will be imperishable and immortal. If
they will not be perishable, many disagreeable things will then
follow, because there will be infinite reproduction, because then
there will be a similar procreation of this generation and there
will be no end to such procreation. For men of the generations
produced by intercourse certainly now have perishable life, but
then they will have the imperishable. And besides, everything
born is necessarily perishable, because reproduction and decay
are opposites but go together. However, if those born then will
be perishable men and will die, if they will not rise again to life,
it follows that their souls always stay separated from their
bodies. This is unsatisfactory, since they are the same type of
creature as the souls of those who will rise again. However, if
they will also rise again, and it will be right for others to expect
their resurrection again, at the same time for everyone who
shares the same nature, let us discuss the gift of the resurrection.

Likewise, Mohammed himself mentions only one day of
resurrection, that is at the end of the world on the day of
judgement, but he makes no mention at all about their
resurrection or their birth.[100] Likewise, there seems to be no
reason why the same people should expect to rise again in the
same way if not everyone should expect to rise again. However,
if anyone says that for those who will rise again there will
indeed be the use of foods and of sexual activities, but not for the
sake of preserving or increasing the body, nor for the increase or
preservation of the human species, but for pleasure alone, which
comes with such actions (since no pleasure for man can be
absent in the final payment of reward, as Mohammed clearly
says in the book of his teaching), it is clear in many ways that he
says so unsatisfactorily. Indeed, firstly because the life of those
rising again will be better ordered than this one which is at
hand.

Moreover, it seems impossible for any disorder to exist in
this life, if someone makes use of foods or sexual activities for
the sake of pleasure, but not because of the need to preserve the

---

[100] This indicates that sexual activity in the Koranic heaven is, indeed, in vain.

body or beget children.   This is also said rationally:[101] for pleasures in the aforementioned actions cannot be the end of those actions. But really, it is more the opposite. Nature has, to this day, attached pleasures to these actions so that animals do not put themselves off from these necessary tasks of nature for the sake of work, which can happen unless pleasures incite the animals. It is, therefore, an unsatisfactory and preposterous state of affairs, if these actions are done solely for pleasures. Therefore, there is no use whatsoever for such things for those who will rise again, whose life is most well set in order, and future happiness will be a lot less concerned with such things. For otherwise, what forbids the other irrational animals from being happy too in the aforementioned actions, which they share with us?

Likewise, if the final blessedness for man is in these actions, as Mohammed clearly seems to say, in favour of what is it now fitting to be restrained from these things and not rather eat and luxuriate by day and night, as we can also be happy in this way? Yet among all men, even amongst the Saracens themselves, it is seen as more honourable to hold back from these things. Moreover, they even have certain observant and self-controlled men whom they praise very greatly.

But since it is foolish to speak with good reasoning to a man completely devoid of intelligence, would it be permitted to both act crazily and ask: if the final blessedness for man lies in such actions, what then will the soul do which is separated before the resurrection, and which can neither eat nor enjoy luxuries?[102] But nor will the angels be able to be blessed, since they will not experience such pleasures.

Likewise, if the final blessedness of man lies in having many wives, and countless mistresses and young women, however can women be happy, unless they have many men? But on the other hand, how can any man be happy, whose wife

---

[101] Rationally: it seems that this is being used ironically.
[102] This rhetorical device serves to emphases the simple and obvious nature of his argument.

has many other men? Therefore, it must be that either the woman is happy and the man unhappy, or the man is happy and the woman and those under her are unhappy. However, how is it possible for anyone to be happy whose whole household, which he loves, is wretched and unhappy? Therefore, it is more rational that both men and women are miserable and unhappy.

Going through these words is just about enough to demonstrate that this law is irrational with regard to the end and the reward that it promises. It is also irrational with regard to many other things which are contained in this, such as something he often mentions, that God swears by a faithful city and by a fig orchard and olive grove. This is clearly revealed in the chapter *At-Tin*, which means, 'fig'.[103] Men swear by their greaters, such as by God or the saints. God, however, not having a greater by whom he could swear, was accustomed to swear by Himself, just as he swore to Abraham, as it is written in the beginning in Genesis. However, to swear by a fig grove or an olive grove is empty and completely irrational. Likewise, he himself forbids wine to avoid drunkenness, as he says in very many places. But since wine of itself is not evil, it would suffice to only avoid drunkenness. But it seems that all Saracens have dubious characters, because none of them can partake of wine moderately or with sobriety, whereby the dissuading of its use necessarily demands that either wine is frankly evil, or that the Saracens are all intemperate.

---

[103] K. 95.1-4

Chapter nine. That the law of the Saracens contains lies.

Ninth one should consider that this law is not the law of God because it contains obvious lies. For God is the greatest and first truth, by whom it is impossible for any lie to be said. In the Koran in the chapter *Jonah* it says, "Who guides to the truth?" And replying it says, "God gives guidance to truth, and he who guides to truth is truth and should be imitated."[104] And after this, "...in truth, anything without God is not suited to be called the law of God, but is called a lie and a fabrication without God." For just as Augustine said, "If just one lie could be found in the Gospel, according to the same reasoning, the whole Gospel is dubious and false."[105] Moreover, the Koran certainly contains many truths that are found in the Gospel and in the law of Moses and in the prophets. But Mohammed himself inserted so many obvious lies of his own, that just about the whole thing should be considered dubious and false and the work of him who is a liar and the father of the same.

However, the lies contained therein are reduced to ten principle types. For he tells lies about himself, about the Christians, about the Jews, about the Apostles, about the patriarchs, about demons, about angels, about the Virgin Mary, about Christ and about God.

About himself, he certainly says that he is the seal and last of all the prophets past.[106] And he commands to be killed whoever after him asserts himself to be a prophet. But the hand

---

[104] K. 10.36
[105] A paraphrase from epistola XXVIII.III, Augustine's *Letters*.
[106] K. 33.40

of the Lord is not so restricted that the spirit of prophesy cannot be given to another after him. And it is not only the fact that Christians and Jews say that there are prophets among them who had the spirit of prophesy after him,[107] but they themselves have also accepted a certain prophet in Babylon, who was called Solem, which means 'ladder', who the Tartars killed, and with him a vast number of Saracens.

Likewise, he says about himself, magnifying himself, as if from the person of God, that if all the men and all the spirits or angels got together, they would not be able to make such a Koran as this is.[108] Therefore either we understand this in the following way, that they could not make one without the help of God. And what amazing thing is it if they could not make this which he himself says he did not make without God? Or we understand this, that nor would they have been able to make it, even if they were helped by God. But this is an obvious blasphemy.

He says about the Christians, that they attribute a partner to God. This is an obvious lie. For all the Christians in the world say that God is very much one God and most single. After this it says in the Chapter At-Tawbah, which means 'repentance', that Christians deify their bishops and arch-bishops and monks, [109] which is false. Moreover, Mohammed said this like a man ignorant of the language of Christendom. For the Chaldean and all eastern Christians call bishops and monks, since they respect them, Rabbi, which means teacher or my elder. But in Arabic, Rabba is the name of God that means 'Lord of all', which is understood to describe God alone, just as it is among us, when we say, "The Lord be with you." Therefore in error does Mohammed say that Christians call these people gods. Likewise, he says the same about the Christians, that they deify Mary.[110] In addition, he puts in the chapter Al-Ma'idah, which

---

[107] Mohammed
[108] K. 17.88
[109] K. 9.31
[110] K. 5.116

means 'table', that Christ excused himself before God about that, because he did not tell the world that his mother was a goddess. But actually, nor do the Christians say this, namely that Mary is a god or a goddess, but they say that she was a most blameless woman. And the Gospel certainly does not call her a goddess, or an angel, but a woman.

Likewise, he puts down in the same chapter, talking about the Christians and Jews, that they are not sons of God nor friends of God. This he demonstrates by the fact that they are punished for their sins (as he says).[111]   However, this demonstration is completely spurious, for the trials of justice are many.   And just as the apostle says to the Hebrews, "He punishes everyone he accepts as a son."[112]   However, both the righteous and the impious are chastised by God. For the Tartars have inflicted many stripes upon the Saracens themselves, even though they do not have the law. [113]

About the Jews, Mohammed says in the chapter *At-Tawbah*, which means 'repentance', that they deify Ezra and say that he is the Son of God.[114] However, this is an obvious lie. For the Jews make no man out to be God, nor do they say there is a Son of God.

Likewise, in the chapter *An-Nisa*, which means 'women', it says that the Jews themselves say they killed Jesus Christ, the son of Mary, the apostle of God.[115] However, this is an obvious lie, for the Jews do not say that Jesus is the Christ, nor that he was the apostle of God. They call him an unjust man, and they themselves say that it was for blasphemy that they killed him.

About the apostles, it says in the chapter *Abraham*, whom they say was the father of Moses, that they testified and said with Christ, that they were Saracens and followers of the apostle Mohammed. But this is also a lie. For Christ and the apostles were six hundred years before Mohammed. For Mohammed

---

[111] K. 5.18, 65
[112] Hebrews 12:6, quoting Proverbs 3:12.
[113] The Tartars do not have the Koran.
[114] K. 9.30
[115] K. 4.157

appeared at the time of Heraclius, who began to rule in the six hundred and twelfth year after the incarnation of our Lord. From where there are not yet seven hundred years since Mohammed was alive. However, there have been over a thousand two hundred since Christ (and the apostles) was born. And how is it that the apostles were able to be Saracens and imitators of Mohammed, to whom it was decreed by God's person (as he himself says in the Koran in the chapter *Al-Qamar*) that he himself would be the first Saracen?[116] Therefore, Islam was started in the beginning by Mohammed. Then the apostles could not have been Saracens, nor imitators of that man whom they preceded by six hundred years. Or if they were Saracens, it is impossible for him to have been the first Saracen.

He asserts the same thing about the patriarchs. For he says in many places in the Koran, that Abraham and Isaac and Jacob and their sons were Saracens.[117] And he says the same about Noah, that he was a Saracen, and that because the flood came over the earth, because he himself declared that they would be Saracens, then they declined. However, this is completely false. For how could Noah have been a Saracen when he preceded Mohammed by two thousand five hundred years? Likewise, Mohammed even says himself that he was the first Saracen in the world. However, it is impossible to say that Noah and Abraham are Saracens because they became Saracens; for this statement is contrary to the Koran, where it is said that Abraham was not Christian nor Jewish, but purely Saracen. Therefore, it is necessary that just as the Saracens were born of Abraham, so the Jews and Christians were born of him and Noah.

And also, the Saracens say that God promised Mohammed that no-one would enter into paradise before him. And after this, God embraced him and led him to heaven. And there he saw men and many women, and he said, "What is this, Lord?" And the Lord said to him, "Do not be amazed, for these are also

[116] K. 54
[117] K. 2.132

imitators of you." However, it is impossible for imitators of Mohammed to exist except through the Koran. But this was not revealed before Mohammed's time, as is mentioned in many of its places, but especially at the beginning. However, the falsity of this invention is something that anyone who has intellect can well consider, and on account of this, should not be turned to such things.

However, in the Koran, there is a special chapter about demons, where it is clearly said that a great multitude of demons, hearing the Koran, were glad and bore witness to the fact that through it they could be saved. [118] Then they also called themselves Saracens and were saved. However, this contains such a great lie that it does not need to be demonstrated with any argument.

However, about the angels, he says that they all worshipped Adam, except the Devil.[119] Likewise he himself says that, when he came to God with Gabriel, he saw in the sky one angel, who was a thousand times greater than the world, and he was weeping for his sins. And he obtained for himself pardon for his sins. He also says many other false things, about which we shall relate at greater length at the end of this work, when we discuss the vision of greatest fiction, which he claims that he saw. Likewise, he seems to say clearly about the angels, that they are corporeal creatures. For it says in the chapter Sad, and in many other places, that the angels were created from fire, but man from the earth.[120] For it says in other places that many of them are in space, as it will be said in what follows.

Then about the Virgin Mary it says clearly in the chapter *Abraham*, that she was the daughter of Abraham. Moreover, it says Abraham was the father of Moses and Aaron. Also, in the chapter *Maryam*, which means 'Mary', it clearly says that Mary, the mother of Christ, was Aaron's sister,[121] and that Moses and

---

[118] K. 72.1-2
[119] K. 2.34
[120] K. 38.76
[121] K. 19.28

Aaron had a certain sister who was called Mary, and that these three were children of Abraham. This is clear in the sixth section. But between this Mary and the blessed Virgin Mary, the mother of Jesus Christ (the Son of God) fall a thousand five hundred years. And indeed, Mary was the first to die in the desert when Moses led the sons of Israel through the desert to the Promised Land. However, nor was Rome then built, but was founded after this at the time of Hezekiah, the Judean king, who lived over seven hundred years earlier. Then Jesus Christ was born of the Virgin Mary after king Hezekiah at the time of the emperor Octavian, more than seven hundred years after Hezekiah. Now at this time, the Romans held a monopoly of power over the world and sent kings into Judea. Whereby even the Jews bore witness that they have no king but Caesar. Also note, that just as Augustine says, Rome was founded in the times of Ahaz, or according to some others, Hezekiah. And at that time, the people of Israel had been living in the Promised Land for seven hundred and eighteen years, of which twenty seven belong to Joshua the son of Nun. Then three hundred and twenty nine belong to the time of the judges, after which kings began to rule there for three hundred and sixty two years. However, seven hundred and fifty two years fall between the time when the foundations of the city were laid up to the birth of Christ, as deacon Paul says in his Roman histories. Therefore, the Holy Spirit allowed Mohammed to adopt such an obvious lie that any man would easily be aware of the deception.

Likewise, he says about Christ, that he is not God nor the Son of God, and that Christ himself did not say this about himself, but humbly excused himself before God, that he never said this to the world.[122] However, this is an obvious lie. For it is written in the Gospel of John that he said that he was the Son of God[123] and then the Jews wanted to stone him as for blasphemy.[124] Moreover, he also said that he is equal to God,

---

[122] K. 5.116
[123] John 5:17-18 and other places.
[124] John 8:59 and 10:31

and the Beginning,[125] which is especially attributed to God alone, and he said, "If you do not want to believe my words, believe the actions." And earlier in the third chapter it was demonstrated that what the Saracens say is impossible - that the Gospel is corrupt - and it was demonstrated that the Gospel that we have and the Old Testament ought to be accepted by them. But even Mohammed himself tries to point out for himself, in the chapter *Al-Kahf*,[126] the authority of the book that was written before the Koran.

After this he says about Christ that he was not crucified and that he did not die, but God will make him die at the end of the world. He also says countless other lies that are contrary to the truths contained in the Gospels and other scriptures, which it would take a long time to recount.

Then about God, he simply asserts that it is in no way possible for Him to have a son, since He does not have a wife.[127] He also repeats this continually, as is needed in the absence of any other strong argument. However, this kind of argument is like if one said that God has no substance because He has no birth, or that He does not live because He does not eat or breathe. Such fantasy is silly, even for men devoid of intellect and reason. For Christians do not attribute to God His Son as from a woman, but as the heat is from the fire, or the brilliance from the sun, and the word from he who speaks. All these things are rightly said to be born, but not from a woman. For the Son of God is brilliance, and the Word of the Eternal Father is coeternal, and of like essence and on equal footing. However, just as heat and brilliance are not separate from the fire, sometimes fire is among us with brilliance but without heat, such as in the light of a street lamp. Then sometimes there is heat without brilliance as there is in molten iron. So also the Son of God was able to become incarnate, and without him the Father or the Holy Spirit would have been incarnate, though the

---

[125] John 10:30 and Revelation 1:8
[126] K. 18.106
[127] K. 6.101

works of the Trinity are indivisible. Thus, again, the Son of God and the Word of God the Father was able to be written in an imperceptible book, so that it could be read by all men and so that His works would be perceptibly seen to be united in the flesh. And indeed, the written book was able to be broken, but the Word of the Lord endures unto eternity. Just as the command of a king who sends his word in a book to the land that is under him, yet the word itself can never be burned, though the book can be burned. Therefore, Christians say that Christ, since he is the Word of God, is the Son of God. Mohammed also said this same thing about him, though he did not know or understand it. For it says in the Koran in the chapter *An-Nisa*, which means 'women', that Jesus Christ, the son of Mary, is the Word of God and the Spirit of God.[128] So why did Mohammed not say that it is impossible for God to have Word or Spirit, since He does not have a wife?

Therefore, it should be asked of the Saracens, as they themselves ask of Mohammed, when he says that Christ is the Word of God and the Spirit from God, whether he speaks about the Spirit or the Word as accidental,[129] which they prefer, or essential, that is, incarnate. Thus not only the Word and Spirit of God is from God, but also the words and spirit of other prophets and other blessed men. And according to this, what he says is not any great praise for Christ whom Mohammed especially wants to place above all men. But nor is it for such a reason (this Spirit) that God speaks about Himself in the plural, as is the case throughout the Koran. However, if he speaks about the born and substantial Word and Spirit of God, in this way, they certainly understand with us as much concerning the incarnation as concerning the mystery of the Trinity.

Likewise, Mohammed says about God in the chapter *Al-Mu'minun*, that if God had a son, the whole world would now be

---

[128] K. 4.171
[129] Accidental and essential: Aristotelian technical terms of distinction between the essential and non-essential.

in danger.[130] For there would be a difference in opinion between them. However, this supposition is absolutely false. For it supposes that it is impossible for God to have a son unless he is unjust and bold and disobedient. However, we say that the Son of God is the Word of God and the knowledge of the Father, through whom all things work. Moreover, the word understood in the mind and the knowledge of the workman is never, in man, divided from its working intellect. Unless Mohammed blasphemes anywhere and says that God disagrees with Himself or says things contrary to His own intellect and understanding.

Likewise, Mohammed says in the chapter *Al-Ahzab*, that God and His angels pray for Mohammed and the Saracens.[131] We should disregard that of the angels. But when does God pray for them? To whom does He pray? To angels, or men, or Himself? But this is a lie, that He prays to Himself, especially according to Mohammed, who denies the incarnation of the Word and recognises no distinction between the persons of the divinity.

However, he also puts in it certain other lies, equally impossible, just as in the chapter *Al-Hashr*, it says as if from the person of God, "If we brought down this Koran on top of one mountain, you would now certainly see it torn by reverence and fear of God."[132] Also just as it says in the chapter *Al-Qamar*, which means 'moon', that the moon was split, and many other things that would take a long time to tell. By these it can be clear to all wise men that that law is not from God, which contains so many, such obvious lies.

However, after this, certain other inconsistencies exist that the Saracens affirm as true, which are brought out from the Koran into the form of explanation. However, they are contained clearly in Mohammed's book of explanations, out of which, since there are many, here I shall mention only a few.

---

[130] K. 23.91
[131] K. 33.43
[132] K. 59.21

One is that it says that the sky was made from smoke. Then that smoke was made from the evaporation of the sea, and the sea from a certain mountain that was called Caph. And that went around the whole globe and supported the sky. It also says that the sun and the moon used to be of equal light and worth, and that there was no difference between night and day. However, one day, it happened that while Gabriel was flying, his wing touched the moon, which was darkened as we now see it.

Likewise, it also says that the rural pig was born out of an elephant's manure, and the mouse from a pig's manure, and the cat from the lion's forehead. However, it is explained in this way. For when Noah was in the ark with his sons and animals, when they withdrew to the latrine, the ark tilted, especially when the elephant was there. And because he was very afraid, Noah asked God's advice. He said, "Go back, and worship his anus towards the hole where manure comes out." When he did this, manure came out at the same time, and with it a great big pig. While the pig's snout was digging in its manure, as it is accustomed, the mouse was born, and began to gnaw at the ark's food supplies. And then they were most afraid. And Noah, asking the Lord, struck the lion on the forehead, and out came a cat through his nostrils. They say that this is also the reason why they say that the flesh of the pig is not lawful.

However, it says again in the same chapter, that God will, at the end of the world, kill every creature, including the angels and archangels, and nothing alive will remain except for God and Death, who is an angel called Adriel. Then the Lord will command Adriel to kill himself. When this is done, the Lord will cry out in a loud voice and say, "Where are the governors and rulers of the world?" And after this, every thing will rise up again.

And again, Mohammed composed a book in which he wrote twelve thousand miraculous words, but to some people wondering and asking whether all those things were true, he replied that only three thousand had truth, but the rest were false. Therefore, when something false is found in the aforementioned book, the Saracens say, "Mohammed did not say that all of it is true, because of those words, but the whole rest of it stands firm in its own strength." I believe the Saracens also do the same in the Koran. For although many lies are revealed in it, yet for the sake of those things in it that contain truth, just as the Word of God is given praise among them. However, a better thing is said for us, as Augustine says, "If only one false word could be found in the Gospel, it would be fair that the whole Gospel be considered worthless and empty and fictitious."

However, I strongly sense that the wise Saracens especially, and those who have the skill of writing, have no faith in the words of the Koran, but turn away from the fiction of its doctrine. However, the sign for this is that these people refuse to openly dispute with other wise men, as I myself learned through experience. And they do not want the Koran itself to be brought out into the public. For it deeply saddens them when it is read by others, and they never want that book to be translated into other languages. However, we know that pure gold fears neither water, nor fire, nor the test. And because of this, Christians, trusting in God's truth, which is most strong and endures unto eternity, freely argue about the Gospel with other nations. They rejoice in disputing with other nations and they rejoice when [the Bible] is read by other nations, and they long for it to be made public to all and translated into other languages. They even point out Christ's suffering not only in private letters, but also in public writings - the suffering that is seen by other nations as a mockery and a disgrace.

CHAPTER TEN. HOW VIOLENT THE LAW OF THE SARACENS IS.

Tenth, we ought to consider that the Koran is not the law of God, for it is violent. Also, as I will say briefly, this law can properly be called a law of slaughter and death, not only because it sends us to eternal death, but because it compels men to believe the things it says with bodily slaughter. Even in the Koran itself, in the chapter *Al-Baqarah*, which means 'cow', it says that there is no compulsion in the law of God, and that the just is now distinct from the unjust.[133] For what compulsion is greater than slaughter? Therefore, the law that forces men in this way is not the law of God. However, the Saracens themselves call it Islam, which means the law of God's salvation, but which should rightly be called (as was said) a law of slaughter and death. And this way was suitable for such a law and law-giver, on fear of bodily death, to agree to a law of eternal death, just as in the opposite way, Christians disregard bodily death and pursue eternal life. Therefore, as Mohammed saw, or rather his teacher the Devil, this law is completely different to the divine law and to the law that is in the Old and New Testaments. He also saw that it disagrees with itself, and that it contains manifest lies, even without any reasoning or miracle. Then when he considered that because of this, there would be many who would contradict it, he equipped Mohammed with the appropriate tool, that is, the sword to kill. And he himself gave the command in the law, that they be killed whosoever opposes this law and does not believe. And because of this, not only is it said in one chapter, but throughout the whole book, like some kind of universal command, 'Kill! Kill!' This path is clearly the opposite to Christ, who commands us to even love our enemies

---

[133] K. 2.256

and pray for those who persecute us and bless those who offend us.[134] But Mohammed, being the forerunner of the Antichrist, has prepared the way in the world for the child of destruction. Just how irrational this way is was made clear in the eighth chapter. For just as Augustine says, an unwilling man can believe with respect to the rest. He who is compelled to believe can also confess with his mouth, but he can hardly be forced to believe in his heart, since the Lord Himself especially seeks the heart from a man, as it says, "Child, show me your heart."

However, Mohammed's uncle was brought to him and said, "What about me, if I do not do this, son of my brother?" Now Mohammed replied to him, "I will kill you, uncle." Then he said, "Nothing else is possible." He said nothing else, and the uncle said, "I will follow you however you wish because I fear the sword, but [only] in tongue, not with my heart." Also, 'Umar ibn Hattab, when he was forced [to believe], said, "Lord, you know that I am only becoming a Saracen because I fear death." The son of abi Balta'a was also made a Saracen by fear of the sword. Whereby he sent letters to Mecca, which some woman hid under her hair, announcing to those in the city Mohammed's arrival, so they would beware of the strength of his teaching.

However, it should be noted that there are four types of those that still cling to Mohammed's deception. The first of these is those who entered Islam through the sword, as was said, and who would even now recognise their own error and by all means come back to their senses if they were not afraid of the sword. Another type of them [who still cling to Mohammed's deception] is those who were deceived by the Devil, thinking lies to be the truth. The third type is those who do not want to depart from the error of their ancestors, but say that they hold on to the things that their fathers held on to. Yet [their fathers] especially left such things,[135] who chose Mohammed's religion, as no doubt a lesser evil, instead of idolatry. The fourth part is

---

[134] Matt. 5:44
[135] Their fathers left behind their fathers' traditions, namely, idolatry.

those who, for the releasing of life[136] and a multitude of women and other permitted things, loved the dirtiness of these things more than the eternity of the world to come, and they agree with these things. They are called the wiser ones among them and have the skill of writing. They do not believe that their law is true or even good. Instead, the violence of the pleasures sedates the reasoning of the discerning, as a wise man says, "As many literary scholars among the Christians do not keep the law of the Gospel, though they believe it to be true and good, they even copy the way of the Koran instead, however much they believe that it errs from the truth. And evidence exists for this matter on both sides. For some Saracens cross over to Christianity, and some Christians become Saracens. Indeed, a Christian would never become a Saracen in death,[137] but in life; but a Saracen becomes a Christian in death rather than in life. Therefore, each of them chooses to die a Christian rather than a Saracen unless they are prevented in some way by the force mentioned above.

There are three most obvious signs for the violence of the aforementioned law, apart from those that have been said before so often, namely, that it so often tells and commands to kill. The first sign is that Mohammed told them that his law would last for only so much time as their temporal power last while they are a force in arms. But just as Chrysostom says, "Such is the nature of truth, that even when it is fought against by many, it grows stronger in power; and conversely, a lie, when it is aided by many, is weakened in itself." Therefore, truth needs help from no temporal authority, and especially not the truth of the Lord, which endures unto eternity. For the law of the Christians grew especially in the time of persecution that lasted for three hundred years, as did the number of believers and the brilliance of the miracles.

This is also a sign of the violence of the law they have; for when they come to teaching, when a teacher of the Saracens shows them the law, he who ought to preach the word is the first

---

[136] Releasing of life: freedom from restrictions of morality.
[137] In death: on his deathbed.

to bear his naked sword and hold it in his hand, so great is the way he teaches, or terrorises from some lofty position. However, Christians do not teach the sword, but carry the cross, showing signs not of violence, but of gentleness, just like the men who are sent by Christ, like sheep in the midst of wolves.

However, the third sign of slaughter and violence is that the Assassins are supported by the Saracens, future killers of men.[138] They promise them eternal life for the doing and completing of this very action, and they send them through the whole world, to craftily kill off the leaders of the world. Moreover, these Assassins hold camps and castles around Mt. Liltum, and they obey the Sultan of Babylon, who is the head of the Saracens. They are also Saracens with laws and order, and are not called Assassins by the Saracens, but Ishmaelites, like the root and tribe of the Saracens, and the foremost defenders and preservers of the law of Mohammed. For they are chiefly trained and supported for this, to carry out murder. Not only the Christians who have the most sacred law detest this wickedness, but also the Tartars, who say that they have no law except natural law. From these things, therefore, it is clear in an obvious way that the law of the Saracens is a law of slaughter and violence. And a thing is violent whose movement is coerced, because no movement of a thing that is moved is mild, as Aristotle says. And from this it is clear that it is not the law of God.

---

[138] Assassins: Nizari Isma'ilis, a Shi'ite branch of Islam. They believed in the infallibility of the word of their Imam (the doctrine of *Ta'lim*). Some of their teachers adapted a policy of terrorism through assassinations.

CHAPTER ELEVEN. THAT THE KORAN IS NOT THE LAW OF GOD, FOR IT IS DISORDERLY.

Eleventh, it must be considered that the Koran is not the law of God, for it is disorderly. For the things that are from God are ordered, as the Apostle says. Moreover, we see this in the works of nature and in the Holy Scriptures. For it is most solidly convincing, not only to Christians, but also to Saracens themselves, that the law of Moses, the prophets and the Gospel are from God. However, they are all orderly. For Moses was solid concerning the order of time and history. Other prophets also came out well ordered with regard to the order of time (since they demonstrated when and under what kings they were) or with regard to the order of history, or to a lesser extent with regard to the order of material. The Gospel also came out well and orderly, in the order of time, history and material. Indeed, it begins with the incarnation and birth of Christ, then continues about his life, teaching and his miracles, and after these it speaks of his death, resurrection and ascension.

However, there is no order of time at all in the Koran. For it does not even say under what kings or according to what time it is. Nor is there historical order. For the first chapter with which it begins is called the opening, or introduction of the book, in which undoubtedly unique way, it began with a prayer and praise of God. It also began without a middle part after the short prayer was written. Then there is the second chapter about the tawny cow that Moses offered, whose history is in Leviticus. However, the third chapter is about Abraham's family, who was the father of Moses. Here he inserts many things about Christ and says that the Virgin Mary was the sister of Moses and Aaron. And then there follows the fourth chapter about women.

However it goes on similarly, with such disorder about other things to such an extent that there is no-one who can restore the reasoning of the order of history or the order of the chapters. And nor is there order to its material. For it never goes through a subject in good order, but it jumps across from one subject to another completely unrelated thought, like something abstract.

Nor is there even any order to its arguments or any demonstration, but every teaching comes form a supposition, and then bases another proposition on its own truth, and from that concludes something else that has nothing in common with the first. It is like that which is continually said by him, that God is greatest and good, and that the Koran is the law of salvation, and God is God, and that there is no other God but God, and Mohammed is a true prophet. However, what conclusion is this; Mohammed is the true servant of God, and that God is God? Also in the chapter *Al-Ma'idah*, which means 'table', it says, "God established for us the house of Al-Haram, it is one of prayer. This is a house of pilgrimmage. There is also a month of fasting for the Saracens. And this is so that you know, that God knows all things that are in heaven and that are on earth, and God knows whatever exists."[139] But who is so senseless that he doubts that God knows everything?

Furthermore, he continually seems to speak like a dreamer, and especially near the end of the book, where his words seem to let him down. For example, in the chapter *Al-Kafirun*, which means, 'heretics', he says (about the Word in relation to [his] word), "Detestable people! I do not worship what you worship, nor do you worship what I worship. You have your law, and I have my law."[140] But any heretic can say this, in order to cut off the material that concerns the inquisition of truth. And nor do I recollect that I found in the whole book even one argument that comes from a justified supposition or an agreeable conclusion.

---

[139] K. 5. 97
[140] K. 109

However, the order of words there is grammatically and rhythmically outstanding. For almost the whole book is metrical and rhythmical. Whereby the Saracens also strongly exult in such a beautiful and ornate style of Arabic speech. They also argue that Mohammed was a true prophet because of this. For he was a completely uneducated man and would not have known how to speak ornately. But as was seen above in the fourth chapter, it was not God's custom to speak in the world[141] or with the prophets in rhythm or verse. Therefore, it is clear in this way, that this law is not from God, since it has no order but that of rhythm and grammar, which is not congruent with God.

---

[141] in the world *or* in rhetoric.

CHAPTER TWELVE. THAT THE LAW OF THE SARACENS IS NOT THE LAW OF GOD, FOR IT IS UNJUST.

Twelfth, it should be considered that this law is not from God, for God is most good, but this law is only good at doing what Dionysus thinks are great things. At any rate, the fact that the law of the Koran is unjust is clear from the Koran itself. For it says in the chapter *Al-Ahqaf*, and in the chapter *Al-Jinn*, which means demons, that the Koran itself is pleasing to demons and they are delighted in the same. However, demons are unjust and evil in their desires; nothing but injustice pleases them. Therefore, the Koran is wicked.

Likewise, the Koran is the source of every evil, such as slaughter, plunder, perjury and the like; things the Koran not only permits, but also commands, as was made clear earlier - especially slaughter. However, it is not a good enough excuse to order the infidel to be killed but not the faithful. For it undoubtedly says that the believer ought not kill the believer, but commands them to kill the unbelievers unless they pay a tribute. Therefore, is the paying of a tribute good enough reason for killing, or not? Surely this is not what the infidel are worth?

Likewise, as it says in many places in the Koran, "There is no greater evil than to attach a lie to God." However, the Koran contains many other lies, even besides those mentioned above in the ninth chapter. Concerning the lies that are contained in it, it turns them all back to God. Indeed, we can show yet many others. For in the chapter *Al-Anfal*, which means 'spoils', it says that some spoils are God's and His apostle's, and they should give God a fifth part of that which they gained.[142] But surely no God is so unjust that He permits plunder so that He may take a fifth part thereof? And surely God is not so poor that He does not have the means to feed His poor and widows, orphans and strangers (about whom it speaks [in the Koran]) unless He allows further plunder? Hence, in order to profit from it, Mohammed, for his own gain, now surely makes God his consort in Evil, being unable to have a consort in good.

Likewise, though the Koran sometimes forbids plunder and perjury and other such evils, yet this prohibition is actually more a permission. For it says, "You shall not do evil things, for they are not pleasing to God. But if you do, He is merciful and compassionate and will easily spare you."

However, concerning plunder, he never made a command to legitimise it, nor do they have such a tradition, but it is enough, in the end, for a Saracen to say, "There is no God but God and Mohammed is His apostle," as was made clear above in the fifth chapter.

Then again, about perjury, it clearly says in the chapter *Al-Ma'idah*, which means 'table', "God will not charge you anything for the cheating of an oath, but its due." As if it says, "Perjury does not bind a man to blame, but to a penalty." And afterwards it adds, "However, for the man's sin, the bringing up of ten poor boys is enough; or [giving away] the same number of robes, or the freeing of one slave. However, he who cannot do these things will fast for three days."

From these words, every evil follows on. For they do not fear to plunder or cheat or commit perjury, or forsake honesty, though the Christian is taught that one should be honest even with the enemy and infidel. However, the Saracens do have an unquestionable type of oath that they do not lightly break, which we shall discuss after this. However, Mohammed says clearly in the chapter *At-Tahrim*,[143] which means 'prohibition', that God had arranged it for him that he would not have to preserve what

---

[142] K. 8.41
[143] K. 66.2

he had lawfully sworn, namely that he would no longer approach a certain Jacobite woman called Maria, and so he committed perjury, the forgiveness for which, as he says, Michael and Gabriel are witnesses. Therefore, that law is unjust that every evil follows.

Moreover, it is unjust because it attaches so many and such great evils and lies to God. Even besides what is mentioned above, it attaches many other lies and silly things. For it says that God excuses Himself from the fact that He sent the apostle Mohammed, a man, not an angel. He also claims that God said that He would have sent angels, but they would not have been able to travel through the world safely. But surely Mohammed was not able to go through the world more safely than an angel? Because if one thinks of angels as good and peaceful men, here there is no doubt that good and peaceful men can go through the world more safely than evil ones.

He also introduces God continually speaking and saying that it was not in some sporty game that He created the world. But who is such a moron that he thinks about the world that God made it as if he were playing a game?

Likewise, Mohammed, being a Saracen man and continually given to intemperance, in the chapter *Al-Nur*, he introduces God saying, "Let us not enter a house of anyone unless we are invited and called, and unless they shout loudly in the market place."[144] He also adds, as if from the person of God, "And after you have gone in and you have finished eating, leave and do not stop to speak with the porters, because it is a nuisance for the prophet, and a shameful thing to speak. But God is not ashamed to speak the truth."[145] However, in short, whatever he wished to do or that would happen, he attached the whole thing to God and commanded it so that it would become so.

Therefore, in accordance with this, every evil thing followed on as if permitted by the authority of law, that is,

---

[144] K. 24.27
[145] K. 33.53

killing, plunder, committing adultery with the wife of Zaid, committing incest with the Jacobite woman Maria, lying, and not keeping the word of his promises. Therefore, this law is indeed unjust that pleases the Devil, and which leads us into many evils. Therefore, it is not from God, who is most good and from whom only good proceeds, but nothing evil.

CHAPTER THIRTEEN. ABOUT THE ESTABLISHING OF THE KORAN, AND WHO THE AUTHOR AND INVENTOR OF THIS LAW WAS.

Since, therefore, it has been demonstrated that the law of the Saracens, namely the Koran, is not from God, it follows that we ask about Mohammed's disciples and the establishing of the aforementioned Koran. Therefore, it is beneficial to know that it is most firmly believed by their scholars and is shown by working intellects, that the Koran's chief author was not a man, but the Devil. He, because of his own hatred, though by God's permission, because of the sins of the people, prevailed to solemnly and effectively set in motion the treachery of the Antichrist. Then the Devil saw that faith in Christ was growing, especially in the eastern parts, and that idolatry was failing, now that Chosroes the Persian king had been defeated together with the idolatry of the Medes, through the most Christian Emperor Heraclius. (He destroyed that tall tower that Chosroes himself built for idolatry out of gold and silver and precious stones.) The Devil also saw that the cross of Christ was now so greatly exalted through Heraclius, and was being exulted even higher. And since the Devil was no longer able to defend a multitude of gods, nor to completely deny the law of Moses and Christ's Gospel, because they had now been published throughout the whole world, he thought out the invention of some law to deceive the world as if it were half way between the Old Testament and the New Testament.

And in order to carry this out effectively, the Devil used a certain man called Mohammed – an idolater, poor in fortune, proud at heart, famous for his deceitfulness. Yet the Devil would certainly have more gladly used a man of good repute, if he would have been allowed, just as he would also have much rather tempted man through another animal that concealed his vices better than a serpent. But God's wisdom did not allow him to use such an animal, nor to take possession of the world through such a man,[146] so that the world itself could easily discern what sort of a law it is that is given through such a law-giver.

Therefore, after Chosroes had been defeated by the aforementioned Heraclius, and the Holy Cross had been brought back to Jerusalem in triumph in the six hundred and twentieth year after the incarnation of our Lord, in the fifteenth year of the Emperor Heraclius, a certain Arab Mohammed appeared. At first, he became rich through a certain widow[147] whom he took in marriage. And after this, he was made the leader of a band of robbers, then broke out in such pride that he also wanted to become king of Arabia. But because they themselves did not accept him, because he was worthless concerning his birth and opinions, he pretended that he was a prophet. Also, though he was oppressed by epileptic weakness and fell continually, so that no-one would be strongly put off believing in him, he would say that an angel was speaking with him. However, after these [episodes] he would give some verses that, as he said, he heard like the sound of a bell ringing in his ears.

And because he was an ignorant and illiterate man, the Devil gave him some of his own heretical allies, both Jewish and Christian heretics alike. For he attached to him a certain Jacobite called Baheyra, and he stayed with Mohammed up to his death. It is even said that Mohammed afterwards killed him. But also some Jews, namely Finhas and Audia called Salon, but afterwards called Abdulla and Selem. They also became Saracens. Also some Nestorians, who agree very closely with the Saracens, since they say that God was not born of the blessed virgin, but only a man, Jesus Christ. And then through his allies,

---

[146] such a man: a man of good repute, as said above.
[147] A merchant woman named Khadija.

Mohammed composed some things for his law, indeed, adopting some things from the Old Testament and some things from the New Testament. At that time the people did not have the Koran.

Yet it is said in their histories, that Mohammed says, "The Koran came down to me in seven men, and whatever is enough is enough." However, they say that these were Naphe, Eon, Omar, Omra, Eleesar, Asir the son of Cethir and the son of Amer. Therefore, we should ask them whether they ever read this openly to Mohammed. And it will be said that they did not, but openly to the elders and according to Mohammed, always in this way. However, it is most sure that these people did not agree with the elder ancestors in the literature that they now hold. This is shown by the fact that the literature of the first group is contrary to that of the second group For from the time of Mohammed, there was no-one skilled in the Koran except 'Abdallah ibn Mas'ud and Zaid ibn Tabit and 'Uthman ibn 'Affan and Habib ibn Cohayb. However, concerning Ali ibn Abi Talib, some say that he knew part, but others say he did not. However, each of them composed a Koran different to the Koran of the others. Then they even fought amongst themselves to the death, not accepting the others' things. After [Mohammed's] death, the people disagreed over the Koran up till the time of Marwan ibn al-Hakam,[148] who put together for them this Koran that they now have. However, he also burned the other Korans. And even then, seven chiefs of cities spoke out against him concerning grammar and particular idioms.

Moreover, we find in their histories that the chapter of divorce used to exceed the chapter of the cow, which at first consisted of two hundred and thirty sentences, but now the whole [chapter] consists of twelve. However, others also say that the chapter of the cow once contained a thousand sentences, though today it contains eighty seven. They also refer to a certain powerful man called Elgas, who took eighty five

---

[148] Marwan ibn al-Hakam: secretary to the Rightly-guided Caliph 'Uthman (Caliph 644-656).

sentences out of the Koran, and added the same number with different meanings. Therefore, how is it true what they say about the Koran, that God says, "We made a warning come down, and we shall preserve it"?

Some histories also narrate that Mohammed died of poison, and the people did not have the Koran. However, when Abu Bakr accepted the position of leader, he ordered that everyone collect whatever he could, and composed this Koran that is in their hands, but he burned the rest.

But in the chapter *Al-'Imran*, it says about the Koran that no-one but God knows its explanation and that those who have deep wisdom say, "We believe in it, for it is all from our God."[149] And actually, there are many things in this book just as scattered and disorderly, as was also made clear above, with the result that they do not speak rationally at all, but in a more deranged way, and they cover up their lies.

It has happened that they agreed that this is the Koran, that they now hold in their hands, and they say that God revealed it to Mohammed and that he wrote according to the mouth of God. However, al-fuqaha, that is, the great teachers and lecturers, have never agreed in its explanation, nor will they agree for all eternity. And this is the case not only between those in the east and those in the west, but the Easterners disagree amongst themselves, as do the Westerners. There are even various divisions in the same schools, even so divided that one condemns another. For some follow Mohammed, and they are many, while others follow Ali, and they are fewer in number and less evil. They say that Mohammed usurped for himself, with tyrannical power, that which was Ali's.

However, some philosophers have rebelled against both and have started reading books of Aristotle and Plato. They have left behind all the sects of the Saracens as well as the Koran itself. When a Caliph from Baghdad learned of this, he built there an academy, a school and a reciting hall, which are most highly valued, and he turned the attention of teaching towards

---

[149] K. 3.7

the Koran. He also ordered everyone who comes from the province of Baghdad to learn the Koran and uphold the burdens and expenses made necessary by its publication. Then he declined, because the Saracens who did not have the Koran were in no way eager to philosophise. For those who engage in the work of philosophy do not consider Saracens to be good, because they despise this Koran for the reasons mentioned above in the eighth and ninth chapters.

CHAPTER FOURTEEN.
CONCERNING THE FICTION OF A
MOST ABSURD VISION.

Fourteenth, one should take not that Mohammed composed a fictitious vision, which is shown in a chapter in the Koran. For it says in the chapter of the sons of Israel,[150] "Praise to Him who made his servant go across in one night from the sanctuary of the Haram (this is a building in Mecca) all the way to the far away sanctuary (that is the Holy Temple in Jerusalem), which we bless", and the rest.

However, the explanation to this sentence is that one day, at an early hour, Mohammed was singing psalms. When he had finished this, he said to the men, "O you men, contemplate, yesterday after I went away from you, Gabriel came to me after the last evening psalms and he told me, "Mohammed, God commands you to visit Him." I asked him, "And where shall I visit Him?" And Gabriel said, "In the place where He is." And he brought for me a beast of burden that was certainly greater than an ass, but less than a mule, and its name was al-Buraq, and he told me, "Get on this and ride to the Holy Temple." Yet when I wanted to get on, the animal shied away. And Gabriel told it, "Stand still, for this is Mohammed, who wants to get onto you." And the animal replied, "Surely I was not sent for him?" Gabriel replied, "You certainly were." And the animal said, "I won't let him get on unless he first supplicates God on my behalf." Then I interceded before my God on the animal's behalf, and I mounted it, and it walked with delicate steps as I sat down, and would put its foot's hoof down onto the horizon of what it could see. And in this way, I came to the Holy Temple in less time than the

---

[150] K. 17 – Al-Isra' (The Night Journey). Quoting verse 1.

blink of an eye. However, Gabriel was with me and led me to a rock in the Holy Temple of Jerusalem, and Gabriel said to me, "Dismount, for you ascend to heaven from this rock." So I dismounted. And Gabriel fastened the al-Buraq beast to the rock with a band and carried me on his shoulders up to heaven. And when we got to heaven, Gabriel knocked on the door, and someone said to him, "Who are you?" He replied, "I am Gabriel." And someone replied, "And who is with you?" He said, "Mohammed." However, the door-keeper said, "Surely you weren't sent for him?" And Gabriel said, "Certainly." So he opened the door for us. And I saw nations of angels, and twice bending at the knees before them, I poured out my prayer. Then after this, Gabriel took me and led me to the second heaven. However, the space between these two heavens was a journey of five hundred years. And as before, he knocked on the door, someone responded to him and it was the same with all of them up to the seventh heaven."

In this seventh heaven, he describes that he saw a multitude of angels. And the size of any one angel was greater than the world by many thousands of times. One of these even had seven hundred thousand heads, and in each head he had seven hundred thousand mouths, and in each mouth, seven hundred thousand tongues, each praising God in seven hundred thousand different ways.

He also saw one angel crying, and asked the reason for his tears. And he replied that he had sinned. Then Mohammed prayed on his behalf. And so, he says, "Gabriel entrusted me to another angel, and that one to another, and so on, until I stood before God and His throne. And God touched me with His hand between the shoulders, so much so that the coldness of His hand pierced though to the middle of the spine in my back. And God said to me, "I have imposed prayers on you and your people." And when I had gone down to the fourth heaven, Moses advised me to go back to take the weight off the people, who could not bear so many prayers. And by a steward who went back and forth to the seventh heaven and then from the seventh back to the fourth, I obtained exemption from ten prayers. Finally, the number of prayers was so greatly reduced that few remained. And although Moses said, "Men will not be able to bear this either", I was embarrassed for the trouble to go up so often, and did not want to go up any more, but returning to the al-Buraq, I rode him, getting off at the sanctuary in Mecca. However, the time it took for all this was less than a tenth part of the night."

However, we have left out more of this vision than we have mentioned. And when Mohammed had told this story to all the tribes, sixty thousand men withdrew from his law. Moreover, when they told him, "Go up to heaven by day so we can see and watch the angels meeting you", he did not acknowledge his lie, but said, "Glory be to my God. I am certainly no more than one among mortal men and an apostle." So, in the chapter of the prophets, he tells about those who ask him to produce a miracle (and this is how they spoke to Mohammed), "You have heard dreams, put together blasphemies, or you speak most poetically. Come to us with at least one miracle, in which way those before you were also sent."[151] He answered (God said), "We destroyed cities not believing before their eyes; will they believe?"[152] How do they hope for miracles from him? He also answered them, "Since those who went before you did not believe in miracles, nor also will you believe in miracles, except by the sword."

Therefore, listen, Mohammedans, if you consider the Koran to be true, for Mohammed himself is the one who affirms that he did no miracle. However, there were more by far of those whom the sword destroyed than those who followed him freely, as was shown above. This fiction of the vision mentioned above alone ought to be enough to confute whatever Mohammed said and did. For as it was said before on many occasions, the Holy Spirit allowed him to be deceived in this way, so that any man can easily recognise the fabrication.

---

[151] K. 21.5

[152] K. 21.6 In this question, there is the assumed knowledge that such cities were shown miracles and yet did not believe. The expected answer is 'no'.

Indeed, now he says unheard of miracles about himself, but sometimes he says that he did no miracle. Sometimes he says that he is only a messenger and a man, then, sometimes he says that he is more than an angel and intercedes for the angels.

Also, how did he need an ass or mule [to get] from Mecca to Jerusalem, when he went up from Jerusalem to the highest heaven even without an ass? How was he able to endure so many splendours of angels in heaven, when he would say that when one angel appeared to him, he would always fall down to the ground, and be shaken, foaming at the mouth, and his hands and feet would be drawn together and caused to bend down? Neither does he claim, in the aforementioned vision, that he was possessed, but he says that he ascended with both body and soul. The sign for this is, that he says that God touched him with His hand between the shoulders, and he felt the coldness right through to the middle of his back's spine. Whereby he supposes that God and the angels have a place in the corporal medium.

CHAPTER FIFTEEN. SIX GENERAL POINTS OF QUESTION IN THE KORAN, AND ABOUT CHRIST'S PERFECTION ACCORDING TO MOHAMMED.

Following on, there are certain doubts and questions in the Koran that must be dealt with, concerning which, since the Saracens cannot restore any reason to them, the Saracens shall not only be frankly called, but also compelled, with convincing proofs, to enter into agreement with the truth.

The first point of question is, what does the Koran want to say when it so often introduces God speaking about Himself in the plural? For it says in *Al-Baqara*, from the person of God, "We told the angels to adore Adam",[153] and the rest. Then after this, it goes on throughout the whole thing, up to the end of the book, sometimes speaking about God in the plural, and sometimes in the singular. For it is a most sure thing for all Christians, Jews and Saracens who can reason, that God is one, the one and only God, and that He cannot have any partner. Therefore, why does He speak about Himself in the plural?

And they cannot say that God speaks about Himself and the angels. For it says there, "We told the angels". Therefore, this speech of God is not of the angels, but to the angels. Likewise, in the chapter *Sad*, it says that they all worshipped Adam except for the Devil.[154] Therefore, it was to all the angels that God said, "Worship Adam". Likewise, in many places in

---

[153] K. 2.34
[154] K. 38.74

the Koran, some such speeches are introduced in the plural concerning God, in the sort of actions that the angels never share with God, such as in the creation of the world and the justification of the sinner. For it is said in many places in the Koran, "Not for sport did we create the heaven and the earth, and the things in between", and "We justified man", and "We sent Mary's son and gave him the Holy Spirit and the Gospel and miracles", and some such things that the angels can never share with God. For the angels were created by God, but they did not at the same time create with God the heaven and earth and the things that are in between.

Nor can the Saracens say that the voice in the plural is that of God and of some other intellect who surpasses the creation, through whom God made all things. For it makes sense that whatever exists apart from God is a creature created by God, and no creature can at the same time be a creator with God.

Likewise, it is impossible to say that God speaks in the plural because of the different qualities that are in Him, such as power, wisdom, justice and such things, which the Arabs call 'Sifat'. For these are not non-essential qualities, nor diversities in God, but they exist in God's very essence. Whereby they do not attribute to God any mixture or plurality, so that through these things God speaks about Himself in the plural. The contrary is the case, because neither man nor angel can speak about himself in the plural because of their diversity, though these non-essential qualities exist in man and angel, and make up a mixture in them.

And actually, such a way of speaking (namely, God, though He is one, speaking about Himself in the plural) is once found written by Moses in Genesis. For in the formation of man, God spoke, saying, "Let us make man in our image." The Jews say that this is the voice of God to the angels. This is certainly contrary to the scriptures, which never say that man was created in the image of angels, but in the image of God. And following after those words, this is what Moses also added, saying, "And God made man according to His own image and likeness, according to the image of God did He make him." Therefore, that voice is of the Father to the Son, or of the entire Trinity to itself. For God is one and single in essence and three in persons.

The Koran would have also been able to say this frankly, if it were not afraid that a distinction of the persons could mean separation of the essence. Because of this, it says in the chapter *An-Nisa'*, "O people of the book, do not be idle in your law, and say nothing but truth about God, that Christ Jesus is the son of Mary and the Apostle of God and the Word of God that He put in her through the Holy Spirit."[155] See, here it names God, and the Word of God and the Holy Spirit. But fearing that, because of this, God's essence would be divided or multiplied, or ended, it immediately adds on, "And do not say three gods, because God is one God." See how boldly it approached that which is especially difficult in the faith, while another says this to John, "The Father, the Word and the Holy Spirit, and these three are one."[156]

Therefore, in the Koran, Mohammed introduces God speaking in the plural without knowing the reason. So the first point of question is clear that we commonly agree with them that God has a Word and Spirit, and so we believe in the single, one true God. And especially about Himself, He speaks in the singular, but because He is three in persons, He sometimes speaks about Himself in the plural.

The second point of question is that the Koran continually mentions the Holy Spirit and the Word of God. Who is that Holy Spirit, and what is that Word of God? Certainly concerning the Holy Spirit, it says in the *chapter Al-Baqarah* from the person of God, "We gave Jesus, the son of Mary, to do signs and clear miracles, and we perfected him through the Holy Spirit",[157] and it repeats this same thing through the whole chapter. Likewise, it says about Mary in the chapter *Al-Anbiya'*,

---

[155] K. 4.171
[156] 1 John 5:8
[157] K. 2.87

"We breathed into her from the Holy Spirit."[158]   And in many other places, it says similar things about the Holy Spirit.

And the Saracens cannot say that it is some creature like a good angel, because it speaks particularly about it, such as saying "one", "holy", "our".   However, there are many holy angels, and all of them are God's.   Therefore, what is the reason that is speaks about it particularly, saying, "our" and "holy"?

Likewise, it would not be a great praise of Christ, whom the Koran intends to commend especially, that God gave him a guardian angel.   For God makes spirits and angels to be our messengers as it says in the Koran in the chapter *Al-Fatir*.[159] Likewise, angels do not sanctify men, but only God, without a mediator, just as only God can forgive sins, as the Koran says.[160] Therefore, the above mentioned Spirit is true God, and the true God is also the one who speaks about the aforementioned spirit, saying, "We gave him the Holy Spirit", and "We breathed from the Holy Spirit."   Therefore, since God's essence is one and single, it cannot be separated or divided.   Yet here we have a giver and the thing given, and the giver says, "We gave", and the one given is called the Holy Spirit, who is said to be given and breathed.   However, between the giver and the one given, there needs to be only a personal distinction, not an essential one.   And here, they are only distinguished by relation to each other.   And this is the only distinction that Christians attribute to the divine persons.

This same question, in its entirety, which we have asked about the Holy Spirit, we can also ask about the Word of God. For it is said in the chapter *Al-'Imran*, "The angels said to the blessed Mary, 'O Mary, God has placed you first above all women.'"[161]   And after this, the angels said, "O Mary, God has a message for you.   He announces to you His Word, and his name is Christ Jesus the son of Mary."[162]   Also, in the chapter *An-Nisa'*,

---

[158] K. 21.91
[159] K. 35.1
[160] K. 3.135
[161] K. 3.42
[162] K. 3.45

it says, "Do not say anything but truth about God, that Christ Jesus is the son of Mary and the apostle of God and the Word of God that He put in her through the Holy Spirit."[163] Therefore, he unequivocally affirms that Christ is the Word of God.

Therefore, it is asked, 'What is this Word of God, a metaphorical word or something personal and real?' If they say that the Word is only a figure of speech and metaphorical, well, they cannot say this. For the Koran and the Gospel speak about him and about one word equally as greatly, but the word of God that is a figure of speech and metaphorical that comes from God is not one, but many. For all good, holy and true words can be called words of God.

Likewise, it would not be an eminent praise of Christ, whom the Koran intends to commend especially, if he is called the Word of God because he speaks the words of God. For not only Christ, but also other prophets have announced God's words, and yet none of them is called the Word of God. For only concerning Christ do the Gospel and the Koran say that he is the Word of God.

However, if the Word is taken literally, it is clear that the Word of God would be everlasting and true God. For just as the word that proceeds from the mouth of a perishable man is necessarily perishable, so the word that proceeds from the everlasting mouth, through which He made the heaven and earth and the things that are in between (as the Koran likes to say) is necessarily everlasting and imperishable.

Moreover, whatever proceeds from God is, essentially, God, and in this way, the Word of God is God. Whereby since the Word differs in some way from the one speaking and holding back the Word, and since in God's essence there cannot be any division or distinction of the essence, it is right that here there is a distinction in the persons and that the Word is distinguished from the speaker only with regard to their relation to each other, as was also said about the Spirit. And this is the Word with which God spoke to make all things that are, as is

---

[163] K. 4.171

also said in the Koran.[164] And according to this, the Koran agrees with the Gospel of John, who says, "All things were made through him."[165]

Therefore, since the word is understood and brought forth intellectually by the one who says it, and because that which is produced by another in the same likeness of king and nature is called a son, it is because of this that we call the Word of God the Son of God. Just as if the sun were to produce from itself such a brilliance of the sort that is a sun, we would call that sun and brilliance the son of the sun.[166]

However, the difference here is that in creatures whose being and essence are different, the nature must be multiplied when the subjects are multiplied.[167] Whereby man also brings forth another man. However, when God, in whom the being and essence are the same, produced the Word from Himself, He did not bring forth another God. For the divine essence is not divided, nor able to be multiplied in any way, because of its utmost perfection and single nature.

Therefore, Mohammed, when he heard Christians saying that God has a son, did not think to consider that it is possible for there to be a son without a mother. And because of this, he added no argument other than that God cannot have a son because He does not have a wife. He also did not think through what David said, whom Mohammed commended so greatly. He said (not about natural sons) that God has many adopted sons, saying, "I have said, you are gods and all sons of the Most High",[168] and not from a woman. Otherwise, Mohammed should also consider with this, that he says that Mary can have a son without a man. But how did he not, in agreement with this,

---

[164] K. 2.117

[165] John 1:3

[166] Son of the sun: the Latin does not have this unfortunate phonetic clash, since it uses the words, 'filium solis'. Luther leaves out the simile altogether.

[167] The nature…multiplied: literally, "…the subjects cannot be multiplied when the nature is not multiplied."

[168] Psalm 82:6

consider that God could have also been able to have a son without a woman?

Therefore, Mohammed spoke the truth when he said that Jesus Christ the son of Mary is also the Word of God, but he did not understand it. For if he had understood it, he would have said, "Because he is the son of Mary, he is true man. Because he is the Word of God, he is true God." For God is not mixed and imperfect like man. God's Word, and understanding of the mind, and skill and doing are not man. But whatever is of God, is God. Whereby the Word of God is God, and the intellect of God is God, and the doing of God is God.

Yet the Koran only takes Christ to be a man. And because of this, after it has said that he is the Word of God, it adds that Jesus is just as Adam is before God, whom He created from the slime of the earth, and said to him, "Be!" But how does this agree with what went before? For though it said that God poured His Word and Spirit into Mary, by whom Christ was born, after this, it voices the opposite, that he is like Adam, whom God formed from the dirt. Therefore, how is it satisfactory that, as it says, God's Word and His Spirit were dirt? And since dirt comes from dirt, are we therefore to suppose that God's nature is also dirt? It is absurd. For His Word and His Spirit would be like some stature that neither thinks nor breathes.

However, the truth is that our God, who is blessed throughout the ages, sees and hears all things, and has the Word born of the virgin Mary and the Holy Spirit, who overshadowed her and fulfilled the humanity of the Word.

However, if they suppose that the Word of God and His Spirit were also in Adam, they will not escape an obvious lie. For if the Word of God had been one with his dirt and flesh, and if the Spirit had filled Adam, then Satan would never have been able to deceive him and would never have led him astray. However, God said to Adam with His Word, "Be!" He made all things with this same Word that was certainly with God from eternity.

And so Christ is true God and the Word of God. For the Word of God is no less than whole God. He is also true man, born of the virgin Mary. And in so far as he is man, he is God's apostle and God's prophet and God's servant. The Koran speaks well where this is concerned, in the chapter *An-Nisa'*, that neither Christ nor the faithful angels will deny that he is God's servant, that is, in so far as he is man.[169] However, in the whole Gospel, it is not found that he Christ says about himself that he is God's servant, in case he leads us to error. But nor does he openly say, 'I am God, and not man', but with true and manifest works, he showed himself to be both true God, and true man.   And because of this, he said, "If you do not want to believe, believe the works."[170] And this is a more effective witness than if he had said this only with words. However, the reason why he did not openly say this before his suffering is mentioned above. Moreover, the apostles and evangelists and other preachers, before and after these things, have said and shown such clear words that the whole world is convinced to believe this.

However, Mohammed, after he had spoken well that Christ is the Word of God, did not stand firm in the truth, but contradicted himself, saying that Christ is not God. However, he said that he excused himself before God, which was revealed above in the ninth chapter to be an obvious lie, this time because he says that Christ said, "Worship my God and your God, my Lord and your Lord."   However, this reasoning has no consistency at all. For in so far as he was true man, he is the true servant of God, as was made clear above.

Then it so happens that Mohammed himself wrote about others, in the chapter of Jonah, saying that some were condemning what they do not understand and what they cannot grasp. Just as he also condemned the mystery of the incarnation, because he did not understand it, nor could he grasp the things written about Christ in the Gospel. And according to the same reasoning, nor did he accept the mystery of the Trinity. For he

---

[169] K. 4.172
[170] John 10:38

could not understand the distinction of the persons that exists even without the distinction of the essence. But what surprise is it, if a worldly man does not grasp God's most excellent mysteries? Therefore, for the third question, these things are enough.

The fourth point of question is that, continually in the Koran, Mohammed praises the Law of Moses, and Job and David, and says that the book of Psalms is brilliant. However, above all books, he commends the Gospel, in which he says there is salvation and guidance.[171] Therefore, the question is why the Saracens do not have or read those books, nor interpret[172] them.

For since Christ commended Moses and the other prophets, Christians[173] (since they did not have these) accepted them from the Jews and translated them into different languages, and they have their original books and read them in schools. Yet the Saracens certainly say that the Jews corrupted the books of the Old Testament, and the Christians corrupted the Gospel and the books of the New Testament. They say that no truth remains in the world except for what is in the Koran. But it is demonstrated above (in the third chapter) that this is false and contrary to the Koran. Likewise, why would such a great prophet, as they claim Mohammed to be, have so highly commended corrupt copies, and why would he have said that salvation and guidance lies in them? Or how could he not have predicted that they would be corrupted in days to come? But rather, he said the opposite, that if the Saracens were ever in some doubt concerning the Koran, they should ask of those who read those books before, that is, the Christians and Jews (he says this in the chapter *Jonah*). However, it was more fitting to say, "Do not believe those who have corrupt books." Likewise, in the chapter *The Imrans* it teaches the Saracens to seek the authority of

---

[171] K. 5.46
[172] ...interpret: *or* translate.
[173] Christians: here referring to gentile Christians.

the law of Moses, saying, "Apply the Pentateuch, if you are true, and read into it", and the rest.

However, the reason that the Saracens do not read the aforementioned books is none other than what the wise men among them know, that the lie of the Koran would be easily recognised if they read the Holy, truthful books. Whereby the Koran also craftily provides for itself and imposes four remedies so that its lie does not stand out clearly. One of these is certainly the command for anyone who says anything contrary to the Koran to be killed, as was revealed above in the fourth chapter. The second says not to argue with men of another sect. The third forbids them to believe such people. For it said in the chapter *The Imrans*, "Do not trust anyone but those who follow our law",[174] even though it says that in the Gospel there is salvation and guidance. It also says that the Saracens are nothing if they do not fill up with law and Gospel. Therefore, they ought to have the Gospel. Fourth, it separates itself completely from them and says, "For me, my law and for you, yours",[175] and the rest. And after this, "You are free from the things I do, and I from the things you do" (this it says in the chapter *Jonah*).[176]

Therefore, if the Saracens were to happily accept the Koran's plan, they would, without doubt, be led to Salvation. For they could have the Gospel and the law of Moses and the other scriptures, especially since the Koran itself continually commends Moses, David, Solomon and the other prophets, and most frequently says that one is not above another. And this was the fourth point of question.

The fifth point of question is, what does Mohammed mean (in the Koran) when he so often says and repeats, writing about himself, "Believe in God and His apostle", "Obey God and His apostle", "Follow God and His apostle"? For we know that faith is owed to God alone, as is honour, divine reverence, the action

---

[174] K. 3.118
[175] K. 109.6
[176] K. 10.41

of obedience and life's following. For He alone is the beginning and end of all things. It is never possible for someone to become His associate or partner. For the Lord said to the Jews in the law of Moses, "You know that alone, I Am."[177] Also, because of this, Elijah says, "If the Lord is [God], go after Him, but if Baal, follow him.[178]

Therefore, it seems from such things that Mohammed does not only give a partner to God, but makes himself His ally and consort. And so it says in the chapter *An-Nisa'*, "God will not spare anyone if they have given Him a partner." However, Christ is neither God's consort nor sharer, but only true God and true man, he was able to say, "Believe in God", and "Believe in me". However, he never said "Believe in God and in me", or "Obey God and me", so that men would not believe him to be God's partner or consort.

The sixth point of question arises when the Koran says many surely excellent things about Christ, but on the other hand, only a few worthless things about Mohammed. Therefore, it is asked, why the Saracens do not follow Christ instead of Mohammed, and the Gospel rather that the Koran? And because opposites contrast more when placed by each other, let us look from the direction and from within what the Koran says about each.

For the Koran says that Christ was announced to his mother through an angel, and sanctified through the Holy Spirit, and conceived by God's virtue, not in the natural way, and born of the most holy Mary, a woman pure above all other women. However, it says no such thing about Mohammed, but that he was an orphan, and a wanderer, led by God.

Likewise, it says about Christ that he is the Word of God, and according to this, there is nothing he cannot know. However, Mohammed was an unsure prophet. For he says that he does not know what will become of him or his followers. He

---

[177] Deuteronomy 32:39, "...videte quod ego sim solus" (Vulgate) 'solus' is not brought out well by many modern English translations.
[178] 1 Kings 18:21

himself also says, "I do not know whether I or you are on the correct path." Whereby it is also held that he said about his father and mother, "If only I knew what they were doing." Likewise, it is held that he himself was deceived by the Jews when needles were put into a wax face and thrown into a well by some women. They also commonly affirm that Mohammed himself died of poison, and of a toxin that some Jewish woman gave him in small portions.

Likewise, Christ most certainly descended from Abraham and Isaac, to whom was made the promise of a blessing and the sought after inheritance. But Mohammed descended through Ishmael, to whom no promise was made, but about whom it was written that he will be a wild man, and his hands would be against everyone and so on.[179]

Likewise, Christ never committed any sin. For God's Spirit and God's Word could not do wrong. However, Mohammed was an idolater and an unscrupulous and forceful murderer, guilty of many other sins from which, as they say, God spared him.

Likewise, Christ performed baffling and useful miracles. For just as it says at the end of the chapter *Al-Ma'idah*, "Christ gave sight to the blind, he cleansed the lepers and raised the dead to life."[180] However, according to the Koran, Mohammed did not perform any miracle. And the things they do say about him are either unsatisfactory or impossible and inconsistent, such as putting together the split moon. Or they are useless, such as the camel talking. Or completely obscure. For he said many things that he did in the dark and at night that he could not show when asked in the day. Whereby they said to him, "You say that you go up to heaven, to God by night; go up by day so that we may see and believe." Christ, however, would do the greatest, magnificent miracles by day, and in public, even as many witnesses were looking on in person, whereby his works are manifest.

---

[179] Genesis 16:12
[180] K. 5.110

In addition, Christ was certainly an excellent teacher, as is said in the Koran. And in the chapter *Al-Ma'idah*, as if from the person of God, it says, "O Christ, consider how I gave you the Holy Spirit, so that you spoke to men while still in your cradles and your earliest years, and I taught you the Book and wisdom, the law of Moses and the Gospel."[181] However, Mohammed was an ignorant teacher and an uneducated man, not knowing another language beside his own, not even knowing the interpretation of his own law. For it says that only God knows the meaning of the Koran.

Likewise, according to the Gospel, Christ was crucified, died, truly rose again, ascended into heaven and sits at the right hand of God. However, the Koran says that he did not die, but that God took him up [to Himself]. Whereby according to both the Gospel and the Koran, and in any event, Christ lives. However, Mohammed is completely dead. But a living helper is better than a dead one.

I leave out those other points of excellence that the Gospel mentions about Christ. Therefore, it is an amazing thing that the Saracens do not follow Christ rather than Mohammed, and the Gospel rather than the Koran, since it is strongly believable that a better law is given by a better law-giver, and is better preserved by God, truthful and uncorrupted, as was demonstrated above in the third chapter.

---

[181] K. 5.110

CHAPTER SIXTEEN. ABOUT THE PERFECTION OF THE GOSPEL ACCORDING TO THE KORAN.

From what is said above, we can easily recognise the excellence of the Gospel according to the Koran. For it was demonstrated before that the Koran is not the law of God, because of the fact that neither the Old nor the New Testament bear witness to this; and because it does not agree with others in its style nor in its opinions; also because it contradicts itself; and because it is not confirmed by any miracle; and because it is irrational; and because it contains manifest lies; and because it is violent; and because it is disorderly; and because it is unjust; and because it is doubtful. For all these things are briefly demonstrated above through the Koran itself. But even so, these things are better demonstrated to those who read that Koran. (Therefore, we can boldly say, "If you do not want to believe us, read the Koran.") However, the opposites to these things appear clearly in the Gospel's teaching. In fact, Mohammed commended Christ especially, as above all prophets who are or who will be, and he praised the teaching of the Gospel above all divine scriptures.

However, we know that nothing is so valid, as a powerful testimony of someone's life or teaching, as praise from those who are trying to give censure. However, Mohammed himself, in the Koran, in the chapter *Al-Ma'idah*, says, "After them we sent Jesus Christ, the son of Mary, the truest prophet, and we gave him the Gospel, in which there is guidance and light and clear truth."[182] And in many places in the Koran, he especially commends the Gospel. In fact, the Gospel manifests itself in

---

[182] K. 5.46 Here, to make better sense, 'terminauimus viam hominum per' has been replaced with 'missimus'.

every place and tongue, always in a most excellent way. Whereby, about the Gospel, I could confidently tell the Saracens, "Whether you do or do not want to believe your own Mohammed about the Gospel, read the Gospel itself."

Also, since God (As it says in the Koran in the chapter *Al-Anfal*, "God wants the truth to be confirmed through His Word, and the control of the heretics severed, so that the truth would be confirmed and emptiness vanish."[183]) made provision and, so that the world should not perish, He arranged for that law, which alone is necessary for absolutely everyone, that law that is the Gospel, to be written in not just one way of speaking, but in Hebrew, Greek and Latin, and after this, to be faithfully translated into every different language.[184] Moreover, at the end of the Gospel, Christ commanded his disciples to proclaim the Gospel to good effect in the whole world. Then so that they could do this, he gave them the grace of tongues and the virtue of miracles.

However, the Koran says for itself that it was given by God in Arabic alone, and the Saracens firmly believe that no-one can know it who does not know the Arabic language. However, it follows that not everyone knows Arabic nor is able to learn it. However, it is written in the Koran, as was demonstrated above, that no-one can be saved but those who live in the law of the Saracens. Wherefore, it could accordingly be asked if God only wants Saracens to be saved, and those who know Arabic. However, the law of Christians, which is written in every language, says that God wants all men to become saved. Therefore, the Saracens (who are only called saved by name, as was said above) and all others who want to be saved by the truth should learn that Christ is necessary for obtaining justification, which comes to us to restore the things alien to us.[185]

---

[183] K. 8.7-8

[184] Suggested word order: "...non in uno idiomate, sed hebraice, graece et latine, et post haec in diversis et omnibus linguis fideliter transferretur."

[185] ...alien to us: those things made alien to us because of the Fall.

Likewise, the Gospel contains the most natural and particular command, "Whatever you would have men do to you, do you likewise unto them." When this one is known, no other command is necessary for loving one's neighbour. Not only does the Gospel contain the truth, but also, as Christian teachers believe, if only one lie could be found in the Gospel, the whole Gospel would be rightly considered dubious, as was determined above in the ninth chapter.

However, the Gospel does not permit any violence. Indeed, it asserts that violence itself, and injury, should be borne patiently, saying, "If anyone beats you with blows to your right cheek, turn the other also; and if anyone takes your cloak from you, do not stop him, but give your tunic also."[186] It also teaches to repay harm endured and hatred with blessing and good will, saying, "Love your enemies. Bless those who hate you, and pray for the wicked and for those who persecute you."[187]

In addition, there is no contradiction to this if some unjust Christians do not keep to these things. For the perversion of unjust men does not prohibit the perfection and truth of the most holy law.

Moreover, the teaching of the Gospel is most well ordered (as was demonstrated above in the eleventh chapter),[188] in its order of time, place, teaching, and material. For it begins with the incarnation of Christ, setting out what happened at his nativity. And at the right time after the nativity, it reveals his teaching and his wisdom. And after these things, it shows his power and miracles, and then his suffering and death, then finally, his resurrection and ascension into heaven. Truly, nothing bad can be found in such perfect teaching, though inconstant and unlearned men say that some blasphemies are contained in the Gospel, such as about Christ's incarnation and suffering, likewise about the mystery of the Trinity. As was said

---

[186] Matthew 5:39-40
[187] Matthew 5:44
[188] eleventh: using suggested change from 'decimo' to 'undecimo'.

above concerning these things, it is written in the Koran that they themselves reject what they do not understand.

To be sure, the law of the Gospel is most trustworthy because it is known at what time, in what place and by which men the teaching of the Gospel was written down. It is also very trustworthy because it is most agreeably and easily understandable, because the things that must be believed are put forward by God's revelation, and are not things that have to be discovered through reason, with the result that more simple people can easily approach it. Likewise, one should know that the Gospel contains nothing that cannot be understood by us who are guided by the lamp of faith. And though it is most true in itself, yet it is not understood by all, but only by the lowly and humble in heart. But the proud and the worldly cannot understand this, whose intelligence holds them to it like a bat's eye to the sun. However, the holy teachers of the Christian faith do not fly like bats in the night, but with attentive eyes like an eagle's, they consider to themselves the rays of truth. Moreover, especially to the advantage of those who are ignorant and looking for reasoning, they interpret the mysteries of faith and truth. And they do not tell those other nations that do not believe (as the Koran does in the chapter *Jonah* and in the chapter *Al-Kafirun* to those who speak against the Koran[189]), "For me my faith, and for you, yours." But they are prepared with a response to whoever challenges the reasoning for the faith and hope that is in them. However, this is appropriate for a wise man – to give rationale and reason to his actions. For otherwise, any fool could condone a law and decide whatever he wanted, and say, "Nothing should be believed that is contrary to those things that are set down by it."

---

[189] K. 10.11 and 41; K. 109.6

CHAPTER SEVENTEEN. ABOUT THE SARACENS' RESPONSE TO WHAT IS SAID ABOVE.

To these things, some of the more superstitious and contentious Saracens try to reply, saying, "We do not say that the Gospel is not from God, since the Koran clearly bears witness to this. Neither do we say that it is imperfect, since it is from God. But the Gospel involves such difficult and excellent things that we cannot do them. For who can love God with his whole heart and love his neighbour as himself? Who can pray for his persecutors and accusers? Who can, with their whole heart, bless those who do them harm?   And the Gospel commands certain other excellent things. Therefore, since it was not a law that was able to be kept, God made provision for the world through a law of salvation; He made lighter commands and gave the world the Koran, which does not contain these difficult things at all, but exists to save men through itself in an easy way." Therefore, they say that the Koran is, generally, more strongly needed to exist for the salvation of the world. And because of this, they automatically call the Koran a law of salvation.

Therefore, they say that the Koran has followed on as if in the place of the Gospel. But this involves an obvious lie. For it is not possible to say that the Gospel was given at a fixed time as, for instance, for the time up to the Koran, and to say after these things that the Koran has taken its place for mankind's salvation, when the Koran clearly bears witness that there is guidance and salvation in the Gospel.

In addition, it cannot be said that after God gave the Gospel, He changed His mind because the world was not able to keep it, and He corrected what was written and moderated the law, since it so happens that God considers our actions. For God knew from the beginning what the Gospel contains and what men are able to bear.

In addition, the Koran itself says that the Saracens are nothing if they do not put into effect the Gospel and the law of Moses, as was said above. However, Christians are only obliged to put the Gospel into effect.

Likewise, how could the Gospel be called perfect if it could not be kept by men according to their abilities? Likewise, if the Gospel is perfect and contains the things necessary for salvation, where is the inconsistency if it contains some difficult resolutions that exist for great perfection, but does not say that they are necessary for salvation?

Likewise, as much as any law is more able to be relaxed, so much less is it, in itself, worthy of any price. Therefore, if the Koran is more able to be relaxed than the Gospel, it is then not as powerful to save. For God did not give a law of lesser effectiveness to make salvation more laborious. And it is decreed in the Koran that demons can also be saved through the Koran itself (as was made manifest above in the seventh chapter), who cannot be saved through the Gospel. Therefore, the Koran is more able to save than the Gospel, therefore, it is also more difficult and laborious.

Likewise, if the Koran is an easier law, it is also more dangerous, since not to observe it will demand a greater penalty. But the Saracens do not keep it - therefore they sin more dangerously – and the fact that they do not keep it nor fulfil it is clear. For they drink wine and get drunk, and they eat foods forbidden them. They do not keep the fast, nor the prayer, nor do they give anywhere near what they are able to, and many other things that someone knows better who gains experience of these things by dialoguing among them. Whether they say that this is easy or difficult, they do not avoid the danger. But actually, Mohammed did try to give an easy law, but he was not permitted to slacken the cane in this way, since many difficult things came in the way. For that law involves a great difficulty when it comes to understanding it. For the Koran says that it is understood by God alone. But the way in which this is irrational was made clear in the eighth chapter.

Likewise, it contains another thing difficult to believe. For it says that the virgin Mary bore Jesus and that God has a Word and a Holy Spirit, things that are also hard in our faith, though [in ours, they are] confirmed by miracles.

Likewise, it is difficult to fulfil because of works like circumcision, and not drinking wine, and avoiding drunkenness- by chick-pea, and other things that involve fasting and prayer and the collection from everyone according to the means given them by God, and many other things, which few Saracens keep.

Therefore, just as it was necessary for the world, that the Gospel's commands be lightened and the somewhat lighter Koran be given, so it could be said again, that another lighter law needs to be given, one that can be observed by men more easily, and so they should blot out the Koran, as they do the Gospel. But if few were saved, the blame would be God's, who gave such a law that men could not keep. But if this is unsatisfactory, then what was said in the beginning must stand, namely that the Gospel is at the same time the most holy law from God and something that can be observed by the world, because Jesus Christ pardons us. Amen.

Preface to the Koran

By Martin Luther, Doctor of Theology and Minister
of the church in Wittenberg [1543].

Translated by Londini Ensis, 2002.

Many people have published decent volumes which discuss the
practices of the Jews of our age, both beliefs and customs, and it
is for this very reason that their lies have been brought forth,
their errors have been brought to light, and their madnesses can
be quite easily disproved. Nor do I doubt that pious minds,
when they bring together the prophetic testimonies with their
deliria and blasphemies, are greatly strengthened in faith and
love for the truth of the Gospel and are incensed with just anger
against Jewish perverseness. For what whole or sensible person
would think that there is as much of the most absurd and
deceitful pretences, or as much madness and sin in Jewish beliefs
and practices, as indeed are detected in them when their secret
rites are revealed by good and learned men such as Lyra,
Burgensus and Margaritha. However, just as in paradise Satan
first deluded poor Eve with his tricks and turned her from God,
in the same way it is certain that afterwards, madnesses of all
peoples were started up by Satan against God's true doctrine.
For because all peoples have offered up human sacrifices, as
examples exist not only of the ancient Greeks and Romans, but
also of more recent peoples, such as Emperor Severus; because of
the Egyptian cats, the Arabian dogs, the lechery of Lampsacus
and then the fact that others developed other marvels; for the
fact that disgraceful things came to be in Cyprus, Thebes and
Egypt and holy practices sprang up elsewhere: it is certain that
all this came to pass as Satan urged on the blinded minds of
men, firstly to show that he is an enemy of God, then to proudly

mock at the weakness of human nature. In the same way also the madnesses of the Jews were started up, when they roused up civil discords after the resurrection of Christ. After the city of Jerusalem had been razed, they rebelled under the leadership of Ben Cosban at the time of Julian when they had begun to build up the temple again. Nor is it any less of a madness that, since they cannot take up arms, they sit in their puddles and slander the Son of God and invent foolish and venomous corruptions of the prophetic accounts. They make up severe rituals, they afflict their own bodies and those of their children, they dream up vague hopes of theirs about dominating the world against the clearly revealed testimonies of the prophets. Indeed, the Devil does not want his pretences to be uncovered nor brought to light nor reproached. But just as the Apostles condemned the errors of the peoples they met, so now the Church of God has a duty to condemn the errors of all peoples who are enemies of the Gospel, so that the glory of God and of his son Jesus Christ may be praised despite the devil and his tricks.

Since the son of God hung on the cross, the whole of creation was a witness, by new and awesome examples, to the death of the God of love, and he was put forth not so much for the Jews, but for the whole world of all times that defied the son of God. Yet even though few were moved, God wanted to make his testimony clear. Thus even though this last age of the world is weighed down by a huge number of idols; Jewish, of Mohammed, and Papal, nevertheless let us speak out the voice of the Gospel and be witnesses to the fact that Jesus Christ, crucified and resurrected, whom the Apostles speak of, is the true son of God and our saviour. And let us feel abhorrence for the errors of all others who fight against the Gospel. I, therefore, in that I have written against the Jewish and Papal idols and will write more given the opportunity, I have thus begun to disprove the destructive beliefs of Mohammed and I will disprove them at greater length.

To come to the point, it is also beneficial to look closely at the actual writings of Mohammed. For this reason I wanted to see the complete writings of the Koran. Nor do I doubt that when other pious and learned men read it, the errors and name of Mohammed will be cursed all the more. For just as the deceptions of the Jews, or madness rather, were better disproved after their secrets had been brought to light, in this way when Mohammed's book is brought to light and all its parts brought together, all pious men will more easily discover the madness and slime of Satan and will be able to disprove him more easily. This reason is what moved me to decide to expose the book.

On the other hand, there are those who fear that feeble minds might be troubled by reading this as if it were a contagion and they might be torn away from Christ. I say this to them. No one in the Church of God is so weak that he does not have this opinion so fixed in his mind that he believes it to be sure thing: that just as surely as he knows that he lives while the senses and functions of his body are active, just as surely as he knows it is day-time when he sees the sun brought up above the earth at midday, so it is plainly impossible for another religion and doctrine to be right about the adoration of God and prayer when, in short, it degrades the prophetic and apostolic scriptures.   Furthermore, the eternal Church is one entity, continuously from Adam, to which God revealed Himself with sure and marvellous testimonies in this very word that He gave to the prophets and Apostles. And so often does He command that He be recognised in that doctrine and that all beliefs which oppose those that came from Him be rejected.   To this one doctrine He binds us, just as it clearly says in Isaiah ch. 59:21, "As for me, this is my covenant with them, saith the LORD; My spirit that is upon thee, and my words which I have put in thy mouth, shall not depart out of thy mouth, nor out of the mouth of thy seed, nor out of thy seed's seed, saith the LORD, from henceforth and for ever."   And Christ said, "If ye abide in me, and my words abide in you, ye shall ask what ye will, and it shall be done unto you."   And Paul said that the Church was built upon the foundation of the Apostles and Prophets. Most firmly condemned, therefore, are all the beliefs of all the peoples that do not know about God or reject his prophets and Apostles. However, Mohammed acknowledges that he has discovered a new religion that disagrees with the prophets and apostles. For this reason, just as you reject the beliefs of the Egyptians who worship cats and the Arabians who worship dogs, so you will detest the fabrication of Mohammed, because he himself openly acknowledges that he does not embrace the teaching of the prophets and Apostles.

If there are those that are so ignorant that they do not have this opinion fixed in their mind, that there is only one true religion that from the beginning was handed down by God in sure accounts through the prophets and Apostles, and if they do not read what Mohammed wrote, but they will hear the Turks or will see them, how ever will they secure themselves against their beliefs? Indeed, idleness is a foul and wicked thing if they do not remind themselves of this very opinion in their daily prayers; if they do not separate themselves from the Jews, the Turks and the heathens in prayer; if they do not think that their God alone is the eternal God, the maker and preserver of all things, who listens to us and will grant us life everlasting, who revealed himself in the prophetic and apostolic scriptures, who sent his son and was willing for him to be the victim on our behalf. And because few people pray in the right way, for that reason the Church is paying the penalty for its incompetence and negligence. But since the penalties are now within sight, let us remember to separate ourselves in prayer (as I said) from the Turks, the Jews, from the heathens, and let us truly call upon God the eternal creator of all things, the father of our lord Jesus Christ crucified for us and raised again. But I will talk about these things more fully.

Daniel and other captives brought the Babylonian king and many others over to recognition of the true God. The Goths, the Henetes and the conquerors of France were converted to the true God by their captives. Now also in the same way perhaps God will call others of the Turks out of their darkness through captives who know about Him. Or he wants those ignorant Christians who are certainly caught in Illyria, in Greece and Asia to be strengthened through them, people who, when they have read the Koran, will be able to defend the Gospel more strongly.

These counter-propositions hold great support: Just as the Church of God is eternal, so too the doctrine of the Church must be eternal. But this book asserts that this creation of Mohammed is new. The Church of God necessarily embraces the Prophets and Apostles: but Mohammed rejects their teaching. Then again, throughout the Church of God from the very beginning, this voice of the Gospel has always been handed down; that the eternal Father wanted the son of God to become the victim for our   sins: but   Mohammed   laughs   at   this   victim   and reconciliation. In the Church, teachings have always stood out about the causes of human weakness, the causes of calamities and death, pre-eminently about the spread of sin after the fall of those who were previously obedient.   Mohammed, just as Epicureus, thinks that these things are empty tales. Then the book itself will present many other counter-doctrines, of which the bringing together in scrutiny and argument will most effectively teach the pious.

This is a matter that must be considered urgently! Especially by us, who teach in the Church. It is something over which we must fight with the armies of the devil in all places. In this our own age, how diverse are the enemies we have seen! The defenders of the idols of the Pope, the Jews, the great many abominations of the Anabaptists, the Servetans and others. Let us also prepare ourselves against Mohammed. Otherwise, what will we be able to say about things we do not know? For this reason, it benefits those who can to read the writings of the enemy, so that they can disprove them more strongly, shake them up and turn them over, so that they can correct others, or at least certainly fortify us on all sides with stronger arguments.

Notes

Notes

Made in the USA
Las Vegas, NV
26 October 2024

10485688R00069